MOVED TO
ACTION

MOVED TO
ACTION

MOTIVATION, PARTICIPATION, AND
INEQUALITY IN AMERICAN POLITICS

Hahrie Han

Stanford University Press
Stanford, California

Stanford University Press
Stanford, California

Printed in the United States of America on acid-free,
archival-quality paper

Library of Congress Cataloging-in-Publication Data

Han, Hahrie.
Moved to action : motivation, participation, and inequality in
American politics / Hahrie Han.
p. cm.
Includes bibliographical references and index.
ISBN 978-0-8047-6224-3 (cloth : alk. paper) —
ISBN 978-0-8047-6225-0 (pbk. : alk. paper)
1. Political participation—United States. 2. Motivation (Psychology)—
Political aspects—United States. 3. Equality—United States. 4. Poor—
United States—Political activity. 5. People with social disabilities—
United States—Political activity. I. Title.
JK1764.H358 2009
323'.0420973—dc22   2009010152

Typeset by Bruce Lundquist in 10/15 Sabon

Contents

Illustrations

TABLES

Acknowledgments

I HAVE MANY PEOPLE TO THANK for help with this project. Writing the book has been an exhilarating, at times frustrating, but ultimately rewarding journey. David Brady, Mo Fiorina, and Jon Krosnick deserve special thanks for their help in the early stages of this project. No one deserves more thanks (or blame) for making me stick with political science than David Brady. From our first discussions about Texas to our many discussions about this project, Brady has been uncommonly generous, not only with advice but also with Sunday afternoon time on his back porch, tickets to Stanford baseball games, and too many lunches and dinners to count. As a mentor, colleague, and friend, he has taught me an enormous amount about research, political science, and life. For that, I owe him an enormous intellectual and personal debt. Luckily we often have contradictory predictions about politics, and I trust I'll whittle away my debt through more wagers over the years. Serendipity put me into contact with Jon, and his work on issue publics eventually laid the foundation for this project. Laying this foundation, however, was no easy task. Jon kindly provided a lot of thoughtful advice, constructive critiques, and time. Mo Fiorina never failed to make incisive comments, modeling the precision and panache that characterize his writing and thinking. I hope to someday think as clearly as he does about the questions—and answers—in my research.

Many others helped shape the project into a book. Paul Sniderman has been amazing in helping me develop ideas for the book and navigate my way through the writing process. He was the first person to make the distinction between the personal and the political, and it took me two years to understand the wisdom of what he was saying. The acuity of his advice never surprises me, but I am repeatedly surprised by how generous someone as busy as Paul can be to a young scholar. Marshall Ganz has been a friend and mentor since college and has always challenged me to look beyond my computer to understand how politics works. He consistently helps me understand and articulate why these questions matter and what participation means in a democratic society. Dennis Chong read the manuscript at several different stages and provided crucial advice each time. His comments about participation among the underprivileged shaped the direction the manuscript ultimately took. Jamie Druckman's comments on several chapters helped me articulate the points I was making much more clearly. Taeku Lee took an interest in the project at a point when I was casting about for help and provided the intellectual direction, encouragement, and support that I needed.

The fifty-eight people who agreed to be interviewed for the Study of Political Pathways deserve special thanks. For confidentiality reasons, I cannot thank them explicitly here, nor can I list the many people and organizations who helped me recruit them. It was a fascinating experience to learn about each person's journey to political participation and inspiring to hear about the commitments these people made to participating in public life. I appreciated the willingness of each interviewee to engage in frank and open discussions and to be probed with sometimes personal and challenging questions.

At Wellesley College, Marjorie Schaeffer provided invaluable research assistance for the Study of Political Pathways. With intelligence, humor, and persistence, she recruited subjects, conducted interviews, and transcribed the audio files (twice!). Emily Sy and Catherine Chen both stepped in at clutch moments to help us finish work on short notice. Lindsay Miller provided able assistance with some literature reviews and data analysis. I am eager to see the great places all of these women will go. All of my colleagues in Wellesley's political science department have enriched my experience as a junior faculty member and given me support as I was finishing this project, especially those in American politics—Tom Burke, Marion Just, Wilbur Rich, and Nancy Scherer. The Knafel Assistant Professorship in the Social Sciences provided generous funding for the project.

In addition, Matthew Levendusky, Chaeyoon Lim, and an anonymous reviewer provided unusually helpful advice on the manuscript in its final stages. Matt and Chaeyoon, along with many other friends from graduate school, manage to make this work actually fun. There are many others whose contributions were invaluable, including Claudine Gay, Simon Jackman, Jeanette Lee-Oderman, Doug McAdam, and Eliana Vasquez. Kathryn Ciffolillo did an excellent job editing the manuscript. It was a pleasure working with Stacy Wagner and Jessica Walsh at Stanford University Press.

Finally, many friends and family inquired politely about my progress through the years and remained supportive even when my responses were muddled. Hilary Conklin and Peter Han get special kudos for reading my turgid academic prose and providing great feedback. As they have been many times in the past, Mom, Dad, Peter, Meredith, Steve, Carol, Hilary, and Scott were just the cheerleaders I needed at crucial times. Kaya was not even a gleam in our eyes when this project began, but now it is she who makes it all worthwhile. More than anyone, I thank Hunter. Who he is and what we share still stuns me every day. For all of that and much more, I dedicate the book to him.

MOVED TO
ACTION

CHAPTER I

The Challenge of Political Equality

IN THE SPRING OF 2006, New Orleans held its first election to choose a new mayor since Hurricane Katrina devastated the city. Only 38 percent of eligible voters participated. When compared with the 46 percent turnout in the 2002 race and the 38 percent who voted in 1998, this 2006 turnout seems unremarkable. But it *was* remarkable because of the large numbers of hurricane refugees who went to great lengths to participate. Six months after floodwaters inundated the city in late August 2005, more than half of New Orleans's 450,000 residents remained in exile, in particular the poorer, less educated African-American residents. Yet 113,591 of these residents found ways to cast ballots for mayor, many of them overcoming huge barriers in order to participate in the political process.[1]

This book unravels the reasons for participation among people like the Katrina refugees by providing insight into the personal commitments that motivate participation among traditionally marginalized people. The book seeks to answer the question, How do people without many educational, financial, and civic resources become engaged to participate in politics? Most research on political participation looks at the whole population and asks, What kinds of people are most likely to participate? Previous researchers have concluded that people who generally care about politics (i.e., are motivated), are able to participate (have resources), and are asked to participate will participate.[2] But they are not the only ones who do. There are many instances, like the 2006 mayoral election in New Orleans, in which people who lack the resources—such as education, money, free time, civic skills—and the general political interest commonly thought necessary do participate. This book explores why.

In the New Orleans mayoral election, the refugees' strong personal commitments to the outcome motivated their participation—regardless of the resources they possessed. For many displaced voters, the stakes in the election were particularly high, as much of the city remained "empty and in shambles." The future of New Orleans seemed to hang in the balance. The final, runoff election came down to a race between an incumbent African-American candidate, Mayor Ray Nagin, and a white candidate, Lieutenant Governor Mitch Landrieu. In the primary election preceding the runoff, Nagin had won easily in the mostly African-American precincts but received less than 10 percent of the white vote. Landrieu, in contrast, had won 30 percent of the white vote and 23 percent of the black vote. Landrieu appeared to be in a better position to woo conservative white voters who had supported other white candidates in the primary.[3]

Voting in this election was no easy task. Many New Orleans citizens had to register to vote from Texas, Arkansas, Tennessee, or other states where they were now living. Citizens eligible for absentee voting had to remember to request and postmark absentee ballots by the designated date. By Louisiana state law, first-time voters must vote in person—so any first-time voter (as well as any voter who missed the early voting deadlines) had to appear at the polling place on Election Day. Activist groups arranged charter buses to transport voters from neighboring states to New Orleans to cast their ballots, but evacuees still had to figure out where to board the buses and spend an entire day traveling to and from the polling centers. The voters who managed to appear at the polling places faced yet another set of challenges. Poorly labeled polling sites, confusing lines at the mega-polling centers, and missing names on the voter rolls led to substantial confusion.[4] Formidable hurdles to voting existed in this election, especially for the thousands of voters who remained scattered throughout the southern United States.

Despite the difficulty of participating in the election, turnout in heavily black precincts actually increased from that in previous elections. Nagin won the race, drawing support primarily from African-American areas as well as from some crossover support from whites.[5] Although numerous voters did not overcome the barriers to voting, many others cared enough about this election to make an extraordinary effort. Dorothy Stukes, chairwoman of the ACORN Katrina Survivors Association, said, "We all want to be a part of the rebuilding and have a voice in selecting someone who wants us back, because there's a lot of people in New Orleans that's trying to keep us out." Similarly, Terry Jackson, a New Orleanian working in Houston to sign up voters, said, "Even though they're making a new start, they want to get involved because they have families still there. Their mothers, fathers, brothers, and sisters are all still there."[6]

This story defies a common narrative in American politics in which underprivileged people are unlikely to participate. In the New Orleans mayoral race, many voters did not fit the conventional profile of well-heeled participants. Most Katrina refugees were not very wealthy or highly educated and thus lacked the resources that existing models assert are the best predictors of political participation. Yet Katrina refugees overcame formidable barriers to voting because they were highly motivated to have their voices heard. Certainly the civic organizations that mobilized participation mattered. Ultimately, however, mobilization needs motivation to succeed. The refugees participated because they cared passionately about who won the mayoral election, as the winner was likely to have a deep impact on their lives and the lives of loved ones. Without their support, it is unlikely that Nagin would have won. The 2006 mayoral election is one of many instances in which a traditionally marginalized group with few resources possessed sufficient motivation to participate and thereby have an impact on the political system.

To understand participation among underprivileged people like the Katrina refugees, I argue that we need a better understanding of how people are motivated. Most political science research assumes that people are motivated through political interest—that is, people must be politicized before they participate, so that they have a general interest in and knowledge about politics. Research shows, however, that the affluent are much more likely to have this interest and knowledge than the disadvantaged.[7] This book argues for a broader conception of motivation that is rooted in personal goals that move people to action. People act not only because they generally care about politics but also because they care about addressing problems in their own lives or living up to a personal sense of who they are. Because a diverse range of people have personal commitments that connect them to politics, this conception of motivation helps us better understand participation among the Katrina refugees. The book analyzes survey data to show that these personal commitments are particularly important for predicting participation among underresourced populations and draws on in-depth interviews with political participants to illustrate commonalities in the way people develop such commitments.

PARTICIPATION AND POLITICAL INEQUALITY

Explaining what motivated the Katrina refugees to participate has implications for political equality in America. The ideal of political equality has always been a key feature of American democracy. From Thomas Jefferson's Declaration of Independence to Martin Luther King Jr.'s famous "I Have a Dream" speech, the notion that "all men are created equal" has been a central part of the American creed. Yet reality has often failed to meet this ideal. Chronic inequality has been an unfortunate reality in American politics for years. Because wealthy individuals participate through campaign donations, for example, they are more likely to gain access to politicians and thereby influence political outcomes. Stories abound of elected officials taking large campaign contributions from wealthy individuals. The media often portray political leaders taking lavish weekend junkets with rich and powerful representatives from corporate America. Scandalous stories of congressional corruption emerge regularly, in which representatives like California Republican Randy "Duke" Cunningham explicitly negotiate with companies to receive bribes in exchange for access to government contracts. Given the plethora of such stories, it is hard not to imagine that wealthy individuals can "buy" influence in government. Indeed, studies of democratic representation have shown that certain people are better represented than others.[8] People who are wealthy or loyal partisans are better represented than those who are not.[9] As the American Political Science Association's Task Force on Inequality and American Democracy recently concluded, "Citizens with lower or moderate incomes speak with a whisper that is lost on the ears of inattentive government officials, while the advantaged roar with a clarity and consistency that policymakers readily hear and routinely follow."[10] Wealthy, well-educated citizens have persistently had more voice in the political process than less advantaged individuals—and, according to the Task Force's report, this trend has only been increasing.

Addressing problems of inequality in representation depends first on addressing problems of inequality in participation. Participation is the mechanism through which certain individuals become better represented than others. In a complex policy-making environment, elected officials are likely to encounter a cacophony of signals about how to act on any given policy issue.[11] Citizens who distinguish themselves in this cacophony have an implicit advantage in influencing legislative decision making.[12] Through voting, citizens communicate their preferences for one candidate or another. By devoting time to writing letters and contacting their elected officials, citizens express preferences for certain policy alternatives. By contributing money, they express support for or dissatisfaction with particular candidates, parties, or organized interests. Elected officials are much more likely to heed the concerns of those whose voices they hear. Only by participating in the political process can citizens make their voices heard.[13]

Historically, nonparticipants disproportionately come from marginalized groups, such as the poor and less educated.[14] Figure 1.1 shows the percentages of people at different education levels who participated in presidential elections from 1948 to 2000. While rates of participation among

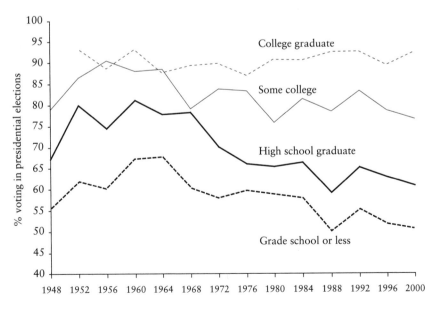

FIGURE 1.1. Rate of voter participation in presidential elections by education level, 1948–2000. SOURCE: Data from the ANES Cumulative Data File.

individuals with at least some college education have remained relatively stable, rates of participation among people with only a grade school or high school education have actually fallen. In 1952 the participation gap between people with a grade school education and people with at least a college degree was about 30 percentage points. By 2000 the participation gap between people with high and low levels of educational resources had increased to more than 40 percentage points. This growing gap poses a central challenge to any effort to remedy inequality in American politics. To ameliorate such inequalities, we need to understand how individuals with few resources become engaged in the political process.

THE NEED FOR A MULTITIERED APPROACH
TO UNDERSTANDING PARTICIPATION

Creating a political system that involves a broad base of people is central to any democracy and presents an ongoing challenge to American politics. History has shown that people of low education, income, and other resources are the most difficult to engage in politics. Increasing participation among this group depends first on understanding the mechanisms that draw these individuals into politics. A broad, single-tiered research strategy that considers the entire population at once may not be appropriate for examining participation within this group. Instead, a multitiered approach that asks whether certain mechanisms are more effective in engaging certain communities—especially the disadvantaged—may be needed. This book thus focuses on a key question: What are the mechanisms by which traditionally marginalized individuals become involved in politics? In other words, what factors draw underresourced individuals into politics?

A rich tradition of research on political participation reveals that people are more likely to participate in politics when the costs of participation are low and the benefits are high.[15] People will not participate if the time and effort it takes to get involved are too costly. Conventional theories of participation argue that people do not participate because "they can't, they were not asked, or they do not want to." Though it oversimplifies the many factors that may enter into a person's decision whether to participate, political scientists generally explain participation by three main factors: resources, recruitment, and motivation.[16]

People who do not participate either cannot (they lack the resources, such as money, time, information, and knowledge about politics), were not asked (they were not recruited), or did not want to participate (they lack motivation).

Most existing empirical research on participation, however, pays minimal attention to the importance of motivation in facilitating participation.[17] In his review of research on participation, Morris Fiorina notes that the dominant, resource-mobilization model of participation focuses primarily on the role of resources and recruitment.[18] In part, this model dominates because many resource-mobilization theorists began by asking why people who have the motivation to participate do not participate. Why do so many people who are politically interested, knowledgeable, and efficacious fail to participate? Taking these motivations as a given, they asked what other factors were important for facilitating participation. Scholars focusing on the civic voluntarism model and its predecessor, the socioeconomic status model, found that individual resources such as education, money, and civic skills help reduce the costs of participation.[19] Mobilization theorists moved beyond individual traits and capacities and focused on the role that recruitment and social interactions play in delivering a contextual supply of information to increase participation.[20] Recruitment helps defray the costs of participation by providing individuals with the information and access they need to participate, and it enhances benefits by providing social rewards.[21] Although these scholars have always acknowledged motivation to be an important factor, they have not theorized much about the way it works. Leading scholars have argued that motivation remains the least understood factor in facilitating participation.[22]

The theoretical focus on resources and recruitment at the expense of motivation has particularly limited our understanding of participation among the underprivileged. People without resources for participation must really *want* to participate if they are to overcome the obstacles posed by their lack of education, money, or skills. Is motivation enough, however? Without much research on what motivates participation, we lack a clear sense of the possibilities. As Figure 1.2 shows, we have a clearer sense of how participation works among certain segments of the population than among others. One dimension of the figure distinguishes between people

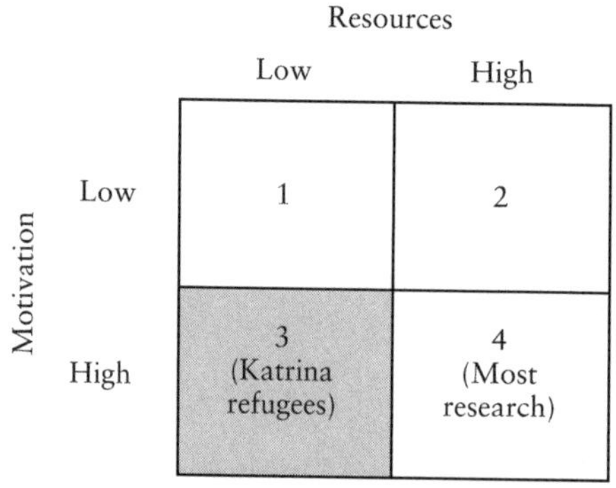

Resources

	Low	High
Low	1	2
High	3 (Katrina refugees)	4 (Most research)

Motivation

FIGURE 1.2 The focus of existing participation research, as shown in a cross-tabulation of individual traits affecting participation.

who have either few or many of the educational, financial, and civic resources that facilitate participation. The second dimension distinguishes between people who have either low or high levels of motivation. We know that people who have both the resources and the motivation for participation (group 4 in Figure 1.2) are likely to participate. Many Katrina refugees participated, however, even though they were not in that group. Many of them lacked resources for participation but presumably were highly motivated (group 3 in Figure 1.2). Yet existing research does little to explain how motivation pushes people who lack resources to participate.

Our incomplete understanding of how the underprivileged become engaged stems partially from a narrow view of what motivation is. Studies of participation often conceptualize motivation as some combination of general levels of political interest, knowledge, efficacy, and party identification.[23] As Kay Lehman Schlozman writes, people are more likely to participate "if they know and care about politics and if they think that their participation would make a difference."[24] Taken at face value, this idea is relatively unsurprising. People who are more politicized in their interests and orientations are more likely to participate. What this conception of motivation lacks, however, is a sense of what people are trying to achieve through their participation—the specific goals that motivate them to take action.

This generalized conception of motivation probably would not have captured the motivation of Katrina refugees voting in the 2006 mayoral election. Many of these voters are unlikely to have scored very high on measures of general political knowledge, political efficacy, or even general interest in politics. Those qualities are most likely to be found in people who also have the educational, financial, and civic resources needed for participation. For example, according to the 2004 American National Elections Study (ANES), 54 percent of respondents who had at least a bachelor's degree said they were "very much interested" in politics, but only 36 percent of respondents with a high school education (or less) said they were "very much interested." And while only 6 percent of respondents with a bachelor's degree or more said they were "not much interested" in politics, 23 percent of respondents with a high school degree or less said so. According to these data, there is a 17- to 18-percentage-point difference in how politicized respondents are, based on how educated they are. Under a generalized definition of motivation, people without many resources do not appear to be very motivated. Yet the underprivileged do get involved, as exemplified by the participation of Katrina refugees. These former residents of the poor neighborhoods hardest hit by the hurricane participated even though they did not have the high levels of income and education commonly associated with high levels of participation. In this specific instance, on this specific issue, these individuals were highly interested, informed, and motivated because they cared deeply about the end being sought.

We need a model of participation that includes the goals that drive people to participate in politics. As Henry Brady writes in his review of research on political participation, "Most models of participation emphasize factors affecting the supply of participation (e.g., political interest, money, time, skills, and education). Little attention is given to those factors, typically the political and social context of an individual, that create a demand for political participation."[25] It is hard to argue with the notion that people with highly politicized interests and identities are more likely to participate than people with apolitical interests and identities. What we lack is a good understanding of what drives individuals to become active in the political system. Or, as John Aldrich has written, "Having even copious resources, strong psychological engagement in politics, and dense networks soliciting one's activity is not, I believe, sufficient to answer, 'Why did she get involved?' What is missing is a domain-specific measure of political preference, of what it is they want to achieve, or, in short, why they are participating. In particular, the individual must care about the political end sought."[26] Although measures of general political interest, knowledge, and efficacy indicate an individual's general orientation toward politics, they are all content-free. They ignore that an important source of motivation may be caring about particular issues.[27] Understanding the importance of motivation to underresourced populations necessitates more precise theories about motivation than those that currently dominate empirical research on participation.

This book argues that personal goals, particularly personal policy commitments, can be especially important for motivating participation among the disadvantaged. Imagine two people, Rahul and Mary.[28] Rahul, the son of two doctors, attended a prestigious private university. He is married and works as a manager in one of the larger private companies in town. He has a strong network of friends from work and school in the area, most of whom are also college-educated professionals. Although politics is not at the forefront of his personal interests, he votes in elections when he can, keeps up with politics enough to discuss it with friends, and has volunteered with local civic organizations in the past when friends have recruited him. Rahul has many of the resources necessary for voter participation: he is educated enough to have basic knowledge about politics and how the political system works; he is embedded in social networks that encourage him to maintain some interest and awareness of politics; he is connected to people who are involved; and he has the financial resources and time to participate when he is so inclined.

Mary is a single mother and former welfare recipient. She has one daughter and pieces together odd jobs to make ends meet. She attends church regularly and grew up in a working-class community. No one in her family and few of her friends and acquaintances have graduated from college. Mary does not regularly read the newspaper or keep up with politics, but she has gotten involved with local politics when an issue directly affected her. The first time she became involved, she and her neighbors organized to protest a landlord threatening to raise rents and push them out of their homes. Unlike Rahul, Mary possesses few of the resources thought necessary for voter participation: she is not very well educated about politics and the political system, she is not part of a social network that encourages interest and participation in politics, and she lacks the financial resources and spare time to devote to politics.

Understanding motivation is particularly important for understanding how people like Mary, who do not have many political, financial, or educational resources, become engaged. For Rahul, there are instances when the costs of participation are low—when friends provide him with all the information he needs to participate, or when his work schedule affords him the time to participate. For Mary, the costs of participation are always high. Finding information about politics and finding the time to participate are consistently a challenge. If both individuals are trying to vote, it is easier for Rahul to figure out where he should go to register, when Election Day is, and where he should be voting. In addition, it is probably easier for him to take the time out of his day to vote. For Mary to overcome these barriers to participation, she must really *want* to participate. Mary participated when she wanted to protect the home in which she and her daughter lived. Regardless of how politicized Mary was, when she had a clear commitment that was personally important to her, she found the motivation to overcome the barriers to participation.

Existing models of participation do a good job of predicting participation among citizens like Rahul who fit conventional profiles of political participants; they are not as good at predicting participation among underresourced individuals like Mary who participate more sporadically. To understand patterns of political participation among traditionally marginalized individuals, we need more nuanced models that account for the sources of motivation for various subgroups of people. This book puts forth such a model by focusing on the personal roots of political action.

THE ISSUE PUBLIC HYPOTHESIS

To study the goals that people bring to politics, I draw on the concept of "issue publics." There is a nearly infinite list of issues people can care about in politics. Philip Converse first coined the term "issue publics" to refer to the different groups of voters who have particular personal concern for certain policy issues.[29] He argued that within the mass public a series of overlapping groups exists, each of which cares about a different issue. In other words, the subset of people who care about environmental issues is the environmental public and the subset that cares about health policy is the health public. A person may belong to both, neither, or just one of these issue publics. Although government handles issues ranging from space exploration to housing subsidies in low-income communities to foreign aid, most citizens care personally about only a small subset of issues, if any. These people have built connections between their personal goals and a specific policy issue.

The issue public hypothesis asks whether personal policy commitments are more important in motivating participation among people at lower levels of education. Conventional models of political participation have not examined the impact of belonging to an issue public. In focusing on the resources (such as education, income, and civic skills) that enable people to participate, the traditional resource-mobilization model overlooks the possibility that people with fewer resources may be drawn into the political process by personal motivations, such as belonging to an issue public. Having a strong personal commitment to policy outcomes is not exclusively the purview of the wealthy and the well educated. Even though many of the displaced New Orleanians lacked political resources, they did care personally about how the city would rebuild. By illuminating the role that personal policy commitments can play in motivating participation and democratic representation, the issue public hypothesis depicts one way that a broader range of people can become engaged in politics.

Like conventional models of participation, the issue public hypothesis accepts the importance of resources, recruitment, and motivation in facilitating participation. Unlike the conventional model, however, it goes beyond the resources necessary for participation and focuses more on the desire to participate. In doing so, it provides an alternate conception of motivation that accounts for the personal goals people are trying to achieve through their participation.

An Alternate Conception of Motivation

The issue public hypothesis deviates from traditional models of participation that conceptualize motivation in only very generalized terms. The hypothesis argues that political motivation is rooted not only in high levels of general political awareness but also in personal concerns that connect politics to people's lives. A mother who is not politically interested may become motivated by concern over her son's schooling; a man who does not regularly read the paper may become motivated when he sees his tax bills steadily rising. These people recognize that political action can help fulfill their personal goals. Motivation in this view is not simply about how interested and aware people are about politics generally; it is about the specific personal life concerns that generate political action.

What differentiates a personal commitment from a political one? As discussed in greater depth in Chapter 2, the crux of the distinction is whether the person has become generally politicized or not. "Politicization" refers to the extent to which a person has expressed a general interest in, knowledge about, and sense of efficacy toward politics. Put another way, politicization is the process of developing a political identity. Much previous research assumes that politicization precedes participation,[30] but this book argues that politicization is not necessary. Instead, personal goals— in particular, personal policy commitments—can be enough. People who have a personal commitment to an issue may get involved even if they are not generally interested in politics. It is important to reiterate that belonging to an issue public, as defined here, indicates a high level of *personal* concern for an issue. Just as most of us consider what happens to our family or loved ones to be of personal concern, members of issue publics consider what happens to government policy to be personally important. Because they care passionately about the political outcomes, they are more likely to participate in an effort to influence those outcomes.

How do these personal commitments lead to political action? The issue public hypothesis conceptualizes motivation as a dynamic process, instead of a set of static individual traits that captures a person's potential to become motivated. This alternate approach builds on a burgeoning body of motivation research in psychology and cognitive neuroscience that shows action to be heavily dependent on the extent to which people have emotional reactions to particular stimuli.[31] Motivation is a process of interpreting the world and making choices about what needs attention.[32] Emotions are critical because they interpret external stimuli and act as signals of what we personally value.[33] Emotions determine and prioritize the external stimuli that require a response. Therefore emotion is fundamental—without emotion, an individual lacks the energizing force necessary for action.[34]

Personal commitments can determine what kinds of things generate emotional reactions. Political stimuli are one of many kinds of stimuli people receive. A campaign advertisement, a canvasser on an individual's doorstep, a story in the newspaper, or a conversation with a friend can all act as political stimuli. In many cases, these stimuli will pass relatively unnoticed in the individual's life. If a person is part of an issue public, however, and cares passionately about a political issue, a related advertisement or conversation may spark an emotional reaction. Given this reaction, the person is then more likely to take political action.[35]

This alternate conception of motivation is thus rooted in the personal goals and commitments that people have. Through daily, ongoing interactions with other people and the surrounding environment, people discover different ways to meet their personal goals. Sometimes they recognize the connection between their personal goals and politics. Once this connection is made (as with issue public members), people value politics more highly in their lives and are thus more likely to act on it.

Participation Pathways

The importance of personal issue commitments to participation leads to a key question: How do people become members of issue publics? How do these connections between personal goals and politics emerge? The tendency in previous research has been to treat the development of motivation as exogenous and to simply study whether or not people are motivated.[36] That research assumes that motivation is the result of idiosyncratic, biographical factors. Some people may be motivated because they were born into highly politicized families; others may be unmotivated because politics was never something discussed at home. Exceptions to this line of reasoning include studies of political socialization, which identify factors that contribute to positive long-term orientations toward politics.[37] These studies focus largely on immutable characteristics of the individual (such as family circumstance or generational cohort) and examine what effect they have on whether the individual matures into a politically active adult.

Conceptualizing motivation as a process necessitates that we better understand how people connect their personal concerns to politics. This book examines the pathways by which fifty-eight people became involved in public life and argues that their pathways have distinct commonalities, despite differences in educational and financial backgrounds, gender, age, region, and race. Some of the people came from highly resourced backgrounds, while others came from relatively underresourced backgrounds. The key finding from this study is that there are systematic patterns to the way personal commitments and the motivation to participate emerge. This counters the traditional assumption that motivation develops in idiosyncratic ways that are dependent on the unpredictable circumstances that shape an individual's life.

The development of political motivation does not have to be idiosyncratic or exogenous to the political system. Studying the pathways people take to political involvement shows that civic and political organizations can play a crucial role in developing issue commitments that motivate action, pushing people to see the connection between their personal goals and political action, and creating conditions that make it more likely people will participate. The commonalities in the pathways that these fifty-eight people described form the basis for a more thorough understanding of the ways that political organizations and institutions of democracy can foster motivation.

Addressing Problems of Inequality

This chapter began by posing a key question about reducing persistent inequalities in American politics: Are the mechanisms that draw individuals without many resources into the political system the same as the mechanisms that draw people with many political resources? And if not, how do they differ? The issue public hypothesis argues that one way traditionally marginalized groups become engaged to participate is through personal commitments to policy outcomes. Such motivation can engage marginalized individuals because personal commitments are distributed more equally through the population than are participatory resources. Belonging to an issue public does not depend on having a lot of money or being very well educated. For example, parents of all types can become engaged in education policy through concern for their children, and citizens of all backgrounds can become engaged in abortion policy through their religious commitments. An individual must simply have a personal commitment to a particular policy issue. It is much harder to endow people from disadvantaged backgrounds with educational, financial, and civic resources. The problem of persistently low or unequal rates of participation can therefore be partly conceptualized as a problem of motivation. Underresourced individuals may not be participating because they are not motivated to participate.

The issue public hypothesis counters the conventional idea that only the wealthy and the well educated are likely to have their voices heard in politics. Because people with high levels of personal concern for an issue are likely to be more motivated to participate in political activities that bear on that issue, they should also be more likely to have their views represented. For example, because senior citizens are especially interested in and active on matters relating to Social Security policy, they influence policy outcomes.[38] Similarly, evangelical churches are often disproportionately active on certain social policy issues such as abortion and gay marriage, and minority groups are often very active around civil rights issues. Because these issue publics participate more actively on these issues, their voices are more likely to be heard.[39]

Making representation more equal can thus be a function of expanding participation. According to the issue public hypothesis, expanding participation is about increasing motivation. Whereas conventional models of participation might argue that inequalities are a function of unequal distribution of resources, the issue public hypothesis argues that inequalities can partially be a function of unequal levels of motivation in distinct segments of society. Civic and political organizations can play an important role in fostering the motivation to participate, and they need to recognize that people who are not politically aware can still be motivated to participate. Political organizations have generally assumed that politically uninterested people without many resources are not likely to be motivated, and thus these organizations ignore certain segments of the population in their mobilization efforts.[40] This approach has left much potential untapped. People who do not fit certain demographic profiles are often not targeted and therefore not mobilized. Mobilization could instead be about reaching out to new groups of people and connecting politics to their personal values, such that they develop the personal commitments necessary for action.

PREVIEWING UPCOMING CHAPTERS

The following chapters unpack the issue public argument. The core idea is that people without many resources for participation are more likely to overcome the barriers to participation when they are highly motivated. Chapter 2 lays the theoretical foundation for the issue public hypothesis by developing a more precise definition of motivation that shows how personal issue commitments can motivate action. The standard resource-mobilization model of participation conceptualizes motivation as a set of individual traits that characterizes an individual's potential to participate. The more politicized a person is, the more potential that person has to participate. Chapter 2 draws on existing research from political science and psychology to develop an alternate conception of motivation in which personal goals animate the emotional arousal necessary for action, regardless of people's general levels of interest in politics. People become energized to take political action when they recognize it as a way of fulfilling their personal goals. Issue publics represent one way people connect their personal commitments to politics.

Chapter 3 defines and describes issue publics in greater depth and shows that people from diverse backgrounds can have personal policy commitments. Research on issue publics is embedded in a broader debate about how political interest and information is distributed in the population. This chapter contrasts the issue public model, which assumes that people specialize in the concerns they have about politics, and the attentive public model, which assumes that people are political generalists. While the former allows for a broad distribution of interest and concern in the population, the latter assumes that only a narrow group of elite are politically aware. By reviewing previous research on issue publics, data on the distribution of issue public members in society, and some of their demographic characteristics, this chapter shows that people of varied backgrounds belong to issue publics. Issue public members are not necessarily better educated or richer than people who do not belong to issue publics; even people with few educational and financial resources have personal commitments that drive political action.

Chapter 4 then shows that having personal policy commitments makes participation more likely, particularly for people with less education. Drawing on observational data from the 1996 American National Election Study and the 1990 American Citizen Participation Study, the chapter shows empirically that people who have strong personal commitments to politics are more likely to participate. These analyses use instrumental variables and two-stage least-squares regression to account for the possibility that personal issue commitments can grow out of participation just as they facilitate participation. The analyses also examine whether the effect of personal issue commitments varies by education level and find that it does. Personal policy commitments are especially important in predicting participation among people with low levels of education. This chapter thus establishes the key links in the issue public hypothesis: the effect of personal issue commitments on participation, and the increasing importance of these commitments as an individual's access to the resources typically linked with participation declines.

Given the importance of personal issue commitments in explaining participation, Chapter 5 explores how they emerge. The chapter draws on the Study of Political Pathways, a set of fifty-eight in-depth interviews with political participants about the processes by which they became involved in politics. Three common themes emerged in the pathways these people described. First, subjects' participation was rooted in a set of personal values, but those values were not enough to predict participation. Most of these people experienced a trigger—a particular life event, a mentor, or an organization—that specifically connected their personal values to political action. Second, the issue commitments of many subjects grew out of or were strengthened by their participation. These commitments were not completely idiosyncratic. Instead (and the third theme), what political organizations did mattered in whether or not people stayed involved. Certain characteristics about individuals' early experiences mattered in escalating their involvement. The systematic patterns in the pathways people take to participation underscore the idea that institutions of democracy—political parties, campaigns, and civic organizations—can play a key role in generating the motivation to participate.

Chapter 6 concludes by discussing alternate ways political organizations can motivate participation. Instead of simply "activating" people who are already motivated, I argue that political organizations can adopt a multitiered approach that recognizes the broad range of people who have the potential to be motivated. Although some people become politically aware of their own accord, many others do not. Political organizations can recognize these differences and focus on connecting people to politics through their personal values and commitments. Through this approach, we can we build a more broadly participatory democracy.

MOTIVATED PARTICIPATION

Woven throughout the argument in this book are hints about the cyclical relationship between political organizations—such as political parties, campaigns, and civic organizations—and motivation. Just as political motivation facilitates participation in political organizations, political organizations have the potential to facilitate motivation. Throughout the 2008 presidential campaign, political observers marveled at Barack Obama's ability to energize participation among a broad base of citizens. Multiple stories emerged about people who had never been involved in politics but nonetheless devoted multiple hours to supporting Obama's run for president. In an online postelection survey conducted with more than 500,000 of the campaign's most energized volunteers, 66 percent of respondents reported never having previously volunteered for a political campaign. Despite being novice political activists, more than 180,000 (or two-thirds) of those who had never before been involved in campaigns said they would like to continue being involved in their communities as part of some Obama-related organization after the election. This unprecedented level of participation among people who would not have been targeted as likely participants surprised the political community. Even those within the campaign seemed incredulous. In a postcampaign interview, reporter Lisa Taddeo describes campaign manager David Plouffe as marveling about the people they were able to engage in politics: "'Do you realize that more than half those volunteers had never been involved in politics before?' David

Plouffe is wide-eyed now, and leaning in. 'More than *half*.' He emphasizes the final word to let the incredulity settle."[41] Since the campaign's end in November 2008, many political analysts have sought to understand how these previously disengaged people became involved.

One technique the Obama campaign used to motivate people was to personalize the campaign for supporters by connecting to the values and local issues that animated their lives. Joy Cushman, an organizer with the Obama campaign and a former activist with the conservative Christian movement, described her experience organizing within the Christian Right: "We were organizing around abortion and prayer in schools, but it was not just focused on Washington, but focused on our local communities. The brilliance of the [conservative] movement was that they realized that for everyday people to be involved, the issues needed to connect to our values and that we needed to have a very local and meaningful way to get involved."[42] The Obama campaign adopted a similar strategy and thus brought to the forefront of politics questions about how political campaigns motivate people to get involved. We know that people are more likely to participate when someone asks them to do so, and this book implies that increasing motivation by connecting to people's personal concerns is one mechanism through which recruitment operates. Some research has studied how political institutions can affect motivation through policy feedbacks, examining the way the structure and design of policy creates communities of people motivated to protect their stake in government.[43] Other research on mobilization has studied the role organizations can play in providing skills and information to potential participants.[44] This book implies that civic and political organizations can play another role by helping generate the desire to participate, thereby influencing who is most active in the political process.

Who gets mobilized, however, depends partially on our assumptions about which individual traits make participation likely. As Steven Schier argues in *By Invitation Only: The Rise of Exclusive Politics in the United States*, political organizations do not reach out to all people equally. Instead, they target their resources by recruiting those who they think are most likely to participate.[45] Given the research finding that people with more resources and more general interest in politics are more likely to participate, political organizations often mobilize them first. This strategy reinforces existing inequalities in society by mobilizing a narrow group of people. Part of what was so surprising about Obama's success in organizing new voters is that he engaged people who were not broadly interested in politics. People who did not have the traits many thought were necessary for participation became activists within his campaign. A broader conception of motivation that includes personal values and commitments implies that more people can be motivated than we thought. Even people who are not generally politicized can be motivated if they connect politics to their personal lives. Changing assumptions made by political organizations about who is motivated has implications for whether the underprivileged get mobilized to participate.

The normative implications of these findings are strikingly important, because they offer a means for reducing inequalities in political participation. The issue public hypothesis presents a theoretical and empirical basis for a more equitable approach to politics. It highlights reasons for political involvement that we previously did not appreciate. People we thought did not or would not get involved in politics in fact do. People who have strong personal commitments to politics are similar in terms of income and education to people who do not. Thus the book specifies a mechanism for popular involvement that does not depend on an individual's income or education level. This lays the foundation for developing a richer understanding of how to shape political participation and remedy persistently low or unequal rates of participation.

Refocusing on the importance of political organizations in motivating people to participate in politics can have implications for American democracy. Democracy necessitates a give-and-take between citizens and political institutions. In representing citizen views, institutions "take" information from citizens and translate it into government action. Much research has focused on the "take." Representative institutions can also "give" back to citizens by shaping the motivation to participate. Given the connection between wanting to participate and finding a voice in politics, the legitimacy of the political system begins, in some sense, with those the institutions seek to mobilize. How political institutions shape citizens affects who participates. Who participates subsequently affects who is represented in the political system and how legitimate a democracy it is. Democratic institutions that mobilize only small groups of people are no more legitimate than a democracy that is responsive to only the concerns of narrow minorities. Recognizing the cyclical relationship between motivation, participation, and political organizations helps us locate democratic legitimacy in a new place. Both the give and the take between political institutions and citizens are necessary to form the rich fabric of democracy.

CHAPTER 2

Theoretical Foundations

WHEN ELENA, a sixty-three-year-old community activist, describes the roots of her political activity, she paints a stark picture:

We actually migrated here from Texas. My mother became a single working mother, and not having been anything other than a housewife when we arrived in California, she found herself having to support two children on her own, and she was forced to actually go out and work in the fields. And in those days they didn't have the child labor laws, so she used to take me with her to work in the fields with her during vacations and weekends and what have you. I was nine years old at that time, and my sister was eleven. So we became farmworkers. . . . Working in the fields was really bad. . . . It was new to me—working in the fields, first of all, and then hearing how the supervisors and the crew bosses were disrespectful to my mother, were disrespectful to older people and to anybody. Sexual harassment was high. My mother was always very careful with me as a young girl—for example, they provided no toilets, so where do you go when you needed to go and relieve yourself? And my mother having to take valuable time off from work just to accompany me to go to the bathroom—so it was that kind of treatment, that kind of situation was difficult for me. . . . It was quite an eye-opener.

These experiences as a farmworker laid the foundation for a lifetime of political activism for Elena. Despite lacking the resources typically associated with political participation—money, education, and civic skills—Elena got very involved in farmworker organizations. Her activism did not stop there, however. Not only has she worked for community-based nonprofit organizations throughout much of her adult life, but she has also been involved with women's rights organizations, the peace movement, immigration rights, labor, and environmental action. She first got involved neither because she was interested in politics nor because she had a sense of her own power as a citizen. Instead, she perceived injustice in her life and the life of people around her. This sense of injustice motivated her to get involved.

The standard resource-mobilization model of participation only partially explains participation among people like Elena. The model depicts participation as primarily a function of the resources people have (such as income, education, free time, and civic skills), whether or not they were recruited for participation, and how generally interested they are in politics.[1] Many people, like Elena, do not possess those resources and are thus less likely to be recruited for participation and be interested in politics.[2] Why do these people participate? Elena participated because she had a strong personal commitment to fixing injustice. In considering motivation, the resource-mobilization model does not take this kind of motivation into account. Instead, it looks primarily at measures of generalized political interest, knowledge, and efficacy. Yet people who do not have the resources for participation very often also lack general interest in politics. What motivates these underresourced individuals to participate?

I argue that personal commitments can be particularly important in motivating underresourced populations to participate. Figure 2.1 broadly categorizes potential sources of motivation. This figure characterizes motivation along two dimensions: how politicized people's psychological orientations and attachments to politics are, and whether or not they have personal commitments to politics. Most previous research has focused on respondents in the bottom row, those who have highly politicized orientations. According to the 1996 American National Elections Study, these respondents also have, on average, statistically higher household incomes, more education, and more civic skills than respondents with low levels of politicization. Given the relationship between politicization and the resources thought necessary for participation, the tendency of research to look only at general indicators of political interest, knowledge, and efficacy as motivation strongly limits our understanding of motivation among the underprivileged. There is a significant group of people, like Elena, who have low levels of politicization but strong personal commitments to politics. In Figure 2.1, this group made up approximately 19 percent (or one-fifth) of the sample. Despite having fewer of the educational, financial, and civic resources for participation, this group participates in

Personal commitments to politics
(issue publics)

		No	Yes
Politicized orientations	Low	% of sample: 15.2 Mean number of participatory acts: 1.6	% of sample: 18.9 Mean number of participatory acts: 2.1
	High	% of sample: 13.0 Mean number of participatory acts: 2.5	% of sample: 23.9 Mean number of participatory acts: 2.7

FIGURE 2.1. Cross-tabulation of general political orientations and personal commitments to politics. SOURCE: Data from the 1996 ANES cross-sectional study. Measurement of the variables used in this figure is described in Appendix B and Chapter 4. Politicized orientations are measured as a composite scale of political interest, efficacy, and knowledge. Respondents in the bottom tercile of politicized orientations are included in the row marked "Low," and respondents in the top tercile are included in the row marked "High." People who belong to at least one issue public are included in the column marked "Yes" for personal commitments, and people who do not belong to any issue publics are in the column marked "No."

an average of 2.1 acts, comparable to the average level of participation in the entire sample (2.2 acts). Previous research, however, has assumed that people in this group are not motivated to participate because they are not generally interested in politics. We have a very limited understanding of how personal goals can motivate participation among this population in the absence of general interest in politics.

To understand how people like Elena are motivated to participate in politics, we need a more nuanced understanding of motivation. This understanding begins with what motivation is and how it works. This chapter delineates an approach to understanding political motivation that draws on disparate lines of research in political science, psychology, and neuroscience. This approach defines motivation as a process in which external circumstances engage with an individual's personal desires to energize participation. Issue publics represent one of many ways in which this process may occur. The goal in this chapter is to provide a broad understanding of motivation that can serve as the theoretical foundation for understanding how membership in issue publics motivates participation. Subsequent chapters will focus specifically on issue publics.

Conceiving of motivation as an interactive process between external stimuli and an individual's personal goals has theoretical foundations in several literatures. Among them is a rich body of work examining contextual effects on participation and research by George Marcus and Ted Brader on the role of emotion in politics.[3] Much of this research has not explicitly focused on political motivation but nonetheless provides crucial insights. Some recent studies by Joanne Miller and Alexander Schuessler that do address motivation also provide useful theoretical grounding.[4] I begin by discussing dominant themes in past research on motivation and then show how these other literatures can provide a rich and nuanced picture of what motivation is and how it works.

THE CHALLENGE

Motivating people to take action is difficult. People will often commit to doing something and renege before actually doing it. Students promise to do their homework, children promise to clean their rooms, friends promise to call you back, colleagues promise to finish the project by Friday—and as our students, children, friends, and colleagues make these promises, many of us think to ourselves, "Fat chance!" The gap between people's expressions of commitment and their actions is large enough that many of us have become accustomed to expecting people to break their word. In some cases, this may be because we know the other person does not really care. Does my child really care how clean her room is? In other cases we know the other person cares, but we still expect their actions to fall short. I know my colleague cares about finishing this project as much as I do, but I still expect her not to do the work necessary to finish by Friday.

The challenge of motivating people to take political action is even greater. For most people, the world of politics seems far more distant than the world populated by friends, children, and colleagues. To use Robert Dahl's famous aphorism, "Politics is a sideshow in the circus of life."[5] Why should people devote precious time and energy to politics? Given families, friends, jobs, household duties, and the myriad demands of life, it is a surprise that anyone has time to participate in politics. Political machinations inside the Beltway, a local hearing on environmental statutes, or even voting understandably take a backseat to a sick child, an important meeting at work, or the opportunity to see a long-lost friend. Research on mass political behavior confirms this. Survey research has consistently shown that most people have little interest in politics and consequently do not take the time to become informed about it.[6]

The challenge becomes even more acute when people have to incur personal costs to participate. Participation is inherently costly because it requires individuals to expend time, energy, and effort to become informed about how to participate and to decide what form their participation will take. How do I register to vote? Which candidate do I support? Where do I vote? What is the best way to contact my elected official? Figuring these things out is harder for some people than for others. People who lack education about the political system or who have few peers involved in politics have to work harder than those who are embedded in civically active social networks or who have received civic education. Likewise, actually participating is costlier for some people than others. People who are paid hourly find it more difficult to take time off from work to vote. People without cars find it more challenging to travel to and from participation sites. For these and other reasons, the costs of participation can be higher for some people than others. The challenge of motivating those people for whom participation is costly is correspondingly greater.

Motivating people to take political action, then, involves not only making people care about politics but also pushing them to follow through on their commitment. Not caring about politics is certainly one part of the participation problem. Yet, as many of us have learned through our own experience, caring about something and doing something about it are not the same thing. People have to care about politics enough to prioritize political action above relaxing in front of the TV or sharing a dinner with friends. Somewhat surprisingly, there are many people who devote substantial time to politics.[7] Many people take political action even as they fail to follow through on commitments to their friends or even at great personal cost to themselves. Why? What moves people to devote their time and energy to politics?

PAST RESEARCH ON POLITICAL MOTIVATION

Past research on political motivation can be roughly divided into two main categories. The first category mostly examines people's potential for participation. This research focuses on general political orientations—how politically interested, knowledgeable, and efficacious people are—to assess how likely they are to participate. The second category questions the substance of motivation and in particular looks at the range of instrumental and expressive goals that motivate people to participate. Although both bodies of research have advanced our understanding of motivation and participation, neither one gives us a good sense of the processes by which goals motivate action, how people make the choice to take action, and how a broader, less elite group of people can be motivated.

Political People Participate

The resource-mobilization model of participation gives limited attention to the question of political motivation. Instead, the model provides a careful explanation of the resources and recruitment mechanisms that make it easier for people to participate. The model's conception of motivation focuses on the individual attributes that make it more likely people will participate, such as political interest, knowledge, and efficacy. People who have these attributes, however, are usually already politicized. In the end, we are left with the sense that people who are more political—in that they perceive politics to be more important in their lives—are more likely to participate. What we lack is an understanding of how people become moved to take political action.[8]

The resource-mobilization model argues that the extent of people's psychological attachments to politics determines the extent to which they want to participate. Rosenstone and Hansen argue that variation in the desire to participate depends "predictably" on people's "interests, preferences, identifications, and beliefs": "People who perceive more at stake in politics—because policies affect them more, identities beckon them more, options appeal to them more, or duty calls them more—participate more in politics."[9] Schlozman makes a similar point in her review of research on political participation: "All else equal, individuals are more likely to participate if they are politically informed, interested, and efficacious, that is, if they know and care about politics and if they think that their participation would make a difference."[10] People who are politicized in their interests, beliefs, or identities are more likely to want to participate.

An overly reductive interpretation of this approach is that more political people are, simply put, more political. People who have already taken time in their everyday lives to express interest in and gather information about politics are more likely to participate. Though oversimplified, this interpretation has had strong implications for how we study and practice politics. Most large studies of participation measure motivation as the extent of a person's political interest, knowledge, efficacy, and party identification.[11] They assume that people who are political in their psychological orientations will be more likely to be political in their actions.

The recent rise of microtargeting in political campaigns is based entirely on the assumption that campaigns should find people who are already politicized in their orientations and simply activate them to participate.[12] The strategy is to "cherry-pick" individuals who likely already support a candidate, a cause, or a party—and then give them information that will activate them to vote.[13] Recruitment becomes less an attempt to move people and more a game of finding people and providing them with information. This implicitly narrows the group of people who are targeted for activation; whereas a more democratic approach could reach a broad-based group of voters, this targeted approach reaches a relatively narrow one.

The second category of research on political motivation focuses on the substance of motivation.[14] What are the goals people pursue through their participation? J. Q. Wilson famously distinguished between "material," "solidary," and "purposive" benefits to participation.[15] Some people participate because they get material rewards, such as political patronage jobs or a lower tax bill at the end of the year. Some benefit from interactions with other people, valuing the social nature of political activity or the increased community status they may derive from their work. Others derive intrinsic rewards from the act of participating itself, such as a sense of fulfillment from doing one's civic duty or a sense of virtue from empowering the disadvantaged. Kay Lehman Schlozman, Sidney Verba, and Henry Brady use a similar typology, distinguishing four major categories of motivations: selective material benefits, social gratifications, civic grati-fications, and collective policy outcomes.[16] Joanne Miller broadens this slightly to identify five motives: self-interest, collective interest, social, value expression (a desire to express one's opinions or values to others), and ego-defensive (a desire to augment or protect one's sense of self).[17] Broadly speaking, all of these studies find that people participate because they have instrumental goals they want to achieve (including material gains or desired policy outcomes), expressive reasons for wanting to participate (including wanting to be a good citizen, express one's values, or protect one's self-image), or relational desires to act with others.

A central debate in this literature asks whether people have instrumen-tal or expressive reasons for participating in politics. This debate arises out of the dominance of economic approaches to understanding partici-pation. Seminal works such as Anthony Downs's *Economic Theory of Democracy* and Mancur Olson's *Logic of Collective Action* introduced a cost-benefit approach to explaining participation.[18] This "rational choice approach" assumes that individuals are rational actors weighing the costs of participation against its benefits. People will participate when the ben-efits outweigh the costs. Downs and Olson both proposed purely instru-mental reasons for participation, leaving scholars with a gaping puzzle: if participation is a purely instrumental act, why would any individual incur the costs of voting, given the minuscule chance of one vote chang-ing any election outcome?

Despite this paradox, dubbed the "paradox that ate rational choice theory" by Fiorina,[19] the rational choice model has become the dominant framework for analyzing participation. Even studies that do not formally employ rational choice methodologies nonetheless use a cost-benefit ap-proach to analyze participation.[20] In part, this approach may be used so frequently because it has been effective in predicting behavior. Given the paradox of participation, subsequent studies sought to incorporate non-instrumental, expressive reasons for participating into their models.[21] These studies argue that expressive motivations are at least as important, if not more so, than instrumental motivations for participation. Scholars such as William Riker and Peter Ordeshook, Morris Fiorina, Einar Overbye, and Alexander Schuessler incorporate this assumption into their models and use the same rational choice framework to analyze its implications. Some were able to predict empirically the conditions under which people were more or less likely to vote.[22]

Limitations of Existing Approaches

Although past approaches have advanced our understanding of what people get out of participation and the traits that political people have, they remain limited in three important ways. First, the study of the goals people are trying to achieve through their participation is largely divorced from the study of the role motivation plays in facilitating participation. Studies of how motivation affects participation relative to resources and recruitment are, as Fiorina puts it, content-free.[23] Second, these studies conflate motivation with the potential to participate. The models ignore the agency people have in making their own choices about whether or not to participate. Third, they implicitly limit participation to a relatively elite group of citizens by assuming that people must have highly politicized orientations for participation. Wealthy, well-educated people are more likely to be politically interested, informed, and efficacious and thus more likely to participate.

In *Mobilization, Participation, and Democracy in America*, Steven Rosenstone and John Mark Hansen write, "People participate because they get something out of it."[24] People derive benefits from participation, whether those benefits are instrumental, social, or expressive.[25] The empirical study of what these goals are, however, rarely ventures into the question of how motivation affects participation. Most empirical studies, such as work by J. Q. Wilson, debate the substance of people's goals.[26] Some theoretical studies, including work by Riker and Ordeshook, examine the capacity of different types of goals to motivate participation, but we have few empirical findings on how instrumental versus expressive goals facilitate participation.[27] In contrast, most empirical studies of how motivation affects participation (such as the classic resource-mobilization model) study motivation without any sense of what benefits people derive. What goals are individuals seeking to achieve through their participation? Psychological research on motivation shows that goals are a central component of motivation—without a goal, the individual lacks a target for any motivational energy.[28] Studies that focus on the psychological attachments that make participation more likely confirm that people who are more interested in politics are more likely to participate. Yet, without goals, we still lack a sense of why they participate.

A second limitation of existing models of motivation is their focus on people's potential for participation at the expense of examining whether people actually want to take action. These models lack theory or mechanisms linking people's inclinations or orientations toward politics with actual action. One distinct feature of many of the benefits people derive from participating or the goals they seek to achieve by participating is that the time and distance between people's political actions and the instrumental rewards they receive are extremely large.[29] As Raymond Wolfinger writes, "Costs and benefits [of participation] are temporally separated by years, if not decades."[30] Imagine an unemployed, financially struggling husband telling his wife that his solution to their problems is to vote for a political candidate with a strong plan to curb unemployment. Although this action may eventually ameliorate some of his economic woes, the potential benefits are contingent on many factors and very far off in time. He may derive more immediate expressive and relational benefits from participation, but those benefits have to compete with the benefits of spending more time on a job search. Political action is constantly competing with other life pressures.

The temporal distance between taking political action and reaping long-term benefits raises the question of how political motivation traverses the gap between people's commitments and their actions. Psychological research has shown that human beings are notoriously bad at curbing immediate appetites for the possibility of long-term gain, no matter how committed they are to their long-term goals. Even if I cognitively know something will be good for me in the long run, I often do not do it. Neuroeconomist David Laibson notes,

We humans are very committed to our long-term goals, such as eating healthy food and saving for retirement, and yet, in the moment, temptations arise that often trip up our long-term plans. I was planning to give up smoking, but I couldn't resist another cigarette. I was planning to be faithful to my wife, but

I found myself in an adulterous relationship. I was planning to save for retirement, but I spent all my earnings.[31]

People often go to great lengths—such as freezing their credit cards, setting up accounts they cannot access, or removing all junk food from their kitchens—to help themselves resist the power of immediate urges. There is no reason to think that politics is any different. In politics, we are asking people to give up their time today in return for potential policy benefits much later.

Given the gap between potential for action and actual action, we need to understand the conditions under which people actually act. General psychological commitments to politics certainly play a role in convincing some people that their precious resources are best spent on politics. It is not clear that those psychological commitments are necessary or sufficient for all people, however. People must choose to act, but models that look only at people's potential for action ignore this aspect of the motivational process. Many people have the potential to participate but do not actually participate. Without examining the goals that push people to choose action, these models strip individuals of the agency they have in making decisions and leave us without a good sense of how people make the choice to act.

A third limitation of existing models is the extent to which they implicitly limit participation to a narrow elite by assuming that politicized commitments are necessary to motivate participation. It is hard to argue with the notion that people with strong political interests and identities are more likely to participate than people with apolitical interests and identities. Are highly politicized orientations a necessary precursor to participation, however? Most previous research assumes that they are. For example, Schlozman and Verba's study of the relationship between economic strain and political behavior presents a participatory model that has five major steps. First, individuals face an "objective" condition that creates strain in their personal lives, such as unemployment. Second, the individuals must perceive that condition as being stressful. Third, the individuals become politicized in their perspectives. This involves the recognition that others may share their condition and that government has the potential to do something about it. Fourth, the individual or group develops policy

preferences related to solving the problem. The fifth and final step is mobilization itself, where the preferences formed in the fourth step direct the
individuals' political activity.[32] In this model, politicization of people's
concerns and psychological orientations precedes participation.

Politicization is not distributed equally throughout society. In most
cases, people with societal advantages such as wealth and education are
those most likely to be highly politicized. Of the respondents featured in
Figure 2.1, only 25 percent of those with low levels of politicization have
at least a bachelor's degree, while 36 percent of those with high levels of
politicization do. Likewise, 38 percent of respondents who are not very
politicized made more than $50,000 a year in 1995, while 48 percent of
respondents who are highly politicized did. Thus there is approximately
a 10-percentage-point gap in education and income between people who
are politicized and those who are not. These differences are statistically
significant, as are the differences between the two groups in terms of how
many civic skills they have. People with more resources are much more
likely to be politicized.

It is not clear, however, that all people who are motivated to participate possess those politicized interests and identities. Elena, for instance,
lacked resources and was not necessarily politicized prior to participation. But she did have strong personal reasons for wanting to get involved
and strong personal ties to the organization that recruited her. For some
people, those intense policy commitments are enough to motivate them
to participate. In other words, the source of some people's political motivation may be personal.

AN EMERGENT APPROACH

Recent bodies of research in political science, psychology, and neuroscience
have provided a dynamic view of motivation. In this view, motivation is
a process, not a state, and one that entails constant interaction between
individuals and their environments. People are moved to action when
their personal goals prompt them to react to external stimuli. Motivation
is the process by which people's internal goals are connected to external
actions—in the case of politics, people choose political action as a way of
fulfilling their personal goals.

What Is Motivation?

A key idea underlying general research in human motivation is that action is at its core an expression of personal value. At any given moment, there are myriad sights, sounds, smells, and other stimuli to which people can react. These stimuli can range from the mundane—an itchy ear, a dry throat, a slight chill—to the consequential, such as uncomfortable disagreement with a loved one, surprise at an unexpected outcome, outrage at a seeming injustice. By choosing to react to these stimuli—by scratching my ear, slaking my thirst, reaching out to my loved one, or acting on injustice—I signal that I value something enough to act on it. If I did not value it enough—if my dry throat or the seeming injustice did not bother me enough—then I could ignore the stimulus or choose not to act.

If action is an expression of personal value, motivation is the process by which we interpret and prioritize stimuli for action. Many different stimuli have the potential to prompt different behaviors—motivation is the process by which those stimuli are evaluated, focused, and prioritized for behavior.[33] The Merriam-Webster dictionary defines motivation as "the act or process of motivating," "the condition of being motivated," or "a motivating force, stimulus, or influence." Following these circular definitions to their root, we find the definition of motive, which is "something (as a need or desire) that causes a person to act," or a "stimulus to action."[34] What constitutes a stimulus to action?

Research finds that humans are stimulated to take action when they have internal goals that are not being fulfilled. In a review of psychological research on motivation, Thane Pittman writes, "Motivation, the activation of internal desires, needs, and concerns, energizes behavior and sends the organism in a particular direction aimed at satisfaction of the motivational issues that gave rise to the increased energy."[35] Unfulfilled "desires, needs, and concerns" can energize a person to take action that will fulfill those desires, needs, and concerns. Motivation, in short, energizes and directs human behavior by identifying and prioritizing personal goals.[36]

Each person has a multitude of personal commitments and goals. Inevitably, some will take priority over others. Emotions play a critical role in the process of prioritization. They are responsible for determining which signals from the environment we ignore and what we prioritize for attention or action. To act, we must first feel the need to act.[37] At any moment, people can respond to their environments in a number of ways. Emotions monitor the environment to determine which and what kinds of responses are most likely to meet a person's personal goals and commitments. Emotions thus provide the crucial link between personal commitments and action. They interpret the world around us and act as signals of what we value.[38]

Given the range of things I could do with my time and energy, how do I decide what deserves the highest priority? The process of interpreting and prioritizing stimuli begins when emotions give meaning to external stimuli.[39] For example, George Marcus notes that a queasy stomach and a cold sweat are meaningless unless we can provide a reason or context for them. A queasy stomach and a cold sweat could indicate illness or fear. To give meaning to these sensations, our emotional systems draw on past experience. When I previously had a queasy stomach and a cold sweat, was I scared or sick? The meaning of queasiness depends on an emotional interpretation of the sensation. Once it has meaning, I can choose whether or not the stimulus deserves attention. If it represents the onset of a cold, perhaps I know there is nothing to do but wait. If it is fear, perhaps I should immediately become more alert. Emotions constantly interpret such sensory information and interpret and prioritize things we see, hear, touch, taste, or smell.[40] In doing so, they influence what actions people will take.

This conception of motivation takes into account the importance of context. Motivation is a dynamic process that constantly changes as the situation changes, and it depends critically on our engagement with the world and people around us. Pittman writes,

A basic characteristic of motivational analyses is the assumption that one salient feature of behavior in situations is that the person is an active participant, an originating striving source with needs, desires, hopes, and fears, and not simply a wet computer through which information enters, is processed, and is emitted as behavior. If a computer analogy must be used, then for one interested in motivation it has to be a motivated computer, a computer with an attitude, with a heart as well as a mind.[41]

Motivation is not a passive state that is bestowed upon a person but instead a state that emerges, shifts, and develops as the person experiences the world. This is consistent with a body of research in political science that recognizes the contextual nature of participation. In *The Social Logic of Politics*, Alan Zuckerman notes that the study of the social context of politics has ebbed and flowed in political science. Classic texts in the study of political behavior recognized the importance of social context in shaping people's behaviors and attitudes.[42] Angus Campbell, Philip Converse, Warren Miller, and Donald Stokes wrote in their study of voters, "Not only does the individual absorb from his primary groups the attitudes that guide his behavior; he often behaves politically as a self-conscious member of these groups, and his perception of their preferences can be of great importance for his own voting act."[43] Attention to these social contexts waned, however, as survey research and its focus on individual units of analysis reached their zenith in political science. Recently, scholars have shown renewed interest in social contexts. Much of this research has focused on the importance of recruitment in facilitating participation,[44] but some has also recognized the role social relationships can play in fostering motivation.[45] Papers by Alan Gerber, Donald Green, and Christopher Larimer and by David Nickerson have shown in a series of field experiments that social norms and social relationships can exert a powerful influence on participation.[46] What are the mechanisms through which social context operates? Scholars such as Jan Leighley, Katherine Tate, and Frederick Harris argue that social context can provide a sense of solidarity, group identification, or other attachments that can form the basis of motivation.[47] Context matters in motivating participation.

Motivation is ultimately a process by which external stimuli are evaluated and prioritized for action. When there is an internal goal that is not being fulfilled, the person is moved to action. In the process of motivation, then, personal goals are connected to external actions. Once particular actions are identified as ways to fulfill personal goals, the person chooses to act.

Focusing on Personal Goals

Conceptualized this way, the motivation to participate in politics can be highly personal. Unlike approaches that argue that political action grows out of people's political interests, this approach argues that political action can also grow out of the personal commitments that prompt emotional reactions to politics. Emotions interpret the world from the subject's point of view—to take action, the subject must feel that the action is personally relevant, important, or valued.[48] This is distinct from believing that something is important for society, or the nation writ large. For instance, I may value political interest as an important characteristic for citizens in a democratic society, but that does not mean I value it in my own life.

What is the distinction between a "personal" and a "political" concern? It may initially seem semantic: people participate when they care about politics, whether we call that a personal concern or a political one. The distinction has more depth than that, however. Two key differences distinguish the two approaches: whether the person has to be politicized prior to participation, and whether the goals the person pursues are anchored in his or her own personal concerns.

The conventional approach to studying political motivation argues that "because policies affect them more, identities beckon them more, options appeal to them more, or duty calls them more," some people will be more likely to participate than others.[49] These people are politicized prior to their participation in the political process. Schlozman and Verba write, "Political activity is more a function of beliefs about politics than of specific personal experiences," and further, political beliefs "are more a function of general social beliefs than of personal experiences."[50] In other words, people participate because they have political concerns, not because they have personal ones. For example, Alex is a lifelong political activist who has worked on a range of different issues. He describes growing up in a highly political family. His mother was a civil rights activist, and "certainly by the age of twelve," he says, "I was reading the *New York Times*, which was my local hometown paper." Alex had a strong general interest in politics, which drove him to attend his first antiwar rally at the age of thirteen and to choose a college that was known for its political activism. For Alex, a general interest in politics preceded and shaped his future involvement. Much research has assumed that politicization has to precede participation, and thus it measures motivation through indicators such as the individual's level of interest in and knowledge about politics—in short, whether the individual has already taken action to learn about politics. While people like Alex would score highly on such measures and thus appear motivated, others may not.

People motivated by personal concerns do not have to be politicized prior to participation. They have personal commitments that prompt emotional reactions that energize action. People have children they care about, parents who are aging, or neighbors they want to get to know. These personal concerns generate emotional arousal and, sometimes, direct behavior toward political action. Elena, for example, had minimal awareness of or knowledge about politics. Yet, she got involved in her community to combat the injustice she perceived as a farmworker. In other words, the nature of the motive that draws people like Elena into civic and political life can be personal, not just political. In this view, politicization of people's concerns happens through their participation—not before.[51] After getting involved in the farmworker movement, Elena became energized about politics and got involved in a range of other political activities. Likewise, a mother attends a PTA meeting out of concern for her son's education and becomes politicized. A constituent makes a frustrating call to his legislator's office about his parents' Medicare options and decides to vote in the subsequent election. People's personal values and concerns put them in positions that may prompt them to become active in politics.

Personal motivations are distinct from political motivations because they are always anchored in issues and concerns localized in a person's life. A central feature of motivational processing is that emotions help people make judgments about importance relative to their individual set of personal goals. In her expansive study of emotions, philosopher Martha Nussbaum argues,

The object of the emotion is seen as important for some role it plays in the person's own life. I do not go about fearing any and every catastrophe anywhere in the world, nor (so it seems) do I fear any and every catastrophe that I know to be bad in important ways. What inspires fear is the thought of damages impending that cut to the heart of my own cherished relationships and projects. . . . The emotions are in this sense localized: they take their stand in my own life. . . . Even when they are concerned with events that take place at a distance, or events in the past, that is . . . because the person has managed to invest those events with a certain importance in her own scheme of ends and goals.[52]

Unless they are anchored to personal goals, emotions have little meaning or significance to the individual.[53] In evaluating external stimuli, emotions implicitly evaluate success and failure relative to a desired end state. This end state may be conscious or not, but it represents a metric against which emotions evaluate the situation. Is this behavior valuable to me? Mary, the single mother described in Chapter 1, describes the distinction as follows: "The rent strike was about what affected me and what I needed to address what was happening in my life. I learned over the years that a lot of activists tend to be . . . people who don't have issues to address in their own lives . . . and they don't connect what's happening with them with politics . . . it doesn't affect them personally." People like Mary and Elena had problems in their own lives that they were trying to fix—an unfair landlord and unjust employment practices. Their attempts to address these issues that were localized in their own lives led them to get involved in politics. Their involvement, thus, was intimately tied to their personal concerns.

Others, as Mary describes, anchor their involvement in general concerns about policy or politics, unrelated to their own lives. Jim, for instance, intermittently volunteers time and donates money to political causes. He has not always been involved in politics and describes the reasons for his involvement as follows:

While I pursued an economics education as an undergrad, I wasn't really [interested in politics]. It wasn't until after I enrolled and I was rooting around and I became more interested in public policy. And I think I was interested as a problem solver, as a young person, but not terribly educated about what was going on in public policy. . . . [A]fter I became a big newshound and interested in public policy, I increased my level of respect for the role of politics as a mechanism to generally get policy done. . . . I think a big piece of it is being very engaged in what's going on in the world. And often seeing the best ideas not really winning out and understanding more and more the mechanisms of politics that lead to certain outcomes and realizing that politics very often trumps the best ideas. And, you know, I think at the same time it was paired a little bit with the sense of hope that, well, politics are trumping the best ideas, but I do think I have some sort of access to be more deeply involved in that political process. I don't think of it so much as a vocational interest or my primary interest, but I do sort of feel this, based on my sense of my own competence and particular skills, [willingness] to get [things done].

Jim finds current events and public policy issues interesting and grounds his political involvement in his general interest in policy and his own sense of efficacy. He describes his interests and motivations without mentioning any personal concerns or goals that drive him to get involved. Previous research has focused primarily on the role these general interests play in driving people's involvement. The approach in this book focuses more on the personal concerns that can also motivate participation.

Personal goals do not always have to be instrumental desires to fix problems in one's own life. They can arise from a multitude of sources. Fighting back against injustice, organizing against an unfair landlord or employer, and seeking better education for one's children are clear examples of personal goals that motivate political action. Personal goals can also be grounded in expressive values, such as citizenship. Heidi says, "I think it's an obligation of every citizen to be involved. I think it's an obligation—at a bare minimum—to be registered and to vote, but where at all possible everyone should be involved in the decisions of our country in an active way. And that was the way I was raised." Others think of participation in terms of personal development. Leah, for example, is a political activist in her twenties who grew up in a relatively privileged community. She locates her motivation to participate in a desire for self-growth, to challenge the boundaries she originally had.

Even though especially my mom and stepfather were really apolitical, my mother, my father, and my stepmother are all psychotherapists. . . . [R]eally rigorous self-analysis and self-work and challenge was a piece of, it was a major value I was raised with. . . . [T]he ultimate goal of life instilled in me wasn't happiness; it was growth. . . . And in the context of racism or white privilege, I was really raised to fear, for self-protection, and I realize that this is a total myth. I don't buy into this, but it was taught to me to fear people of color for self-protection because they were seen as dangerous. And so, when I realized that that fear was based in this mythic hateful system, and that I could do the self-work to begin to transform that system, that was very much in line with the values I was raised with.

Although she did not have an explicit problem in her own life she was trying to solve, Leah grounds her motivation in a personal commitment to self-growth.

Unlike previous studies of motivation that have struggled to untangle the relationship between instrumental and expressive goals, this approach argues that the distinction is unnecessary. Nussbaum distinguishes the concept of personal value from traditional conceptions of self-interest, in which individuals take action only for purely instrumental ends. To describe an individual's complex scheme of goals, Nussbaum draws on the ancient Greek concept of *eudaimonia*, an individual's sense of "a complete human life . . . inclusive of all to which the agent ascribes intrinsic value." When emotions make judgments about which stimuli are most important or most relevant for attention, the stimuli do not have to be "tools or instruments of the agent's own satisfaction"; instead, "they may be invested with intrinsic worth or value [and] loved for their own sake."[54] For example, some people participate in politics because it helps their businesses get more government contracts, while others participate because it makes them feel good to do their civic duty. An individual's sense of value can include things that are instrumentally and intrinsically valuable.

In his study of political activists, Nathan Teske goes one step further and argues that a single act can simultaneously be about fulfilling one's personal goals and helping others. Altruism, the desire to help others, falls into a murky area on the continuum between instrumental and expressive goals. Teske argues that forcing these distinctions is unnecessary:

What these activists said and how they accounted for themselves and their motivations, I contend, calls into question the idea that moral and ethical concerns in politics are simply or solely about something "other" than self. Their language helps to show us how some of the most profoundly held moral concerns, although about actions that affect others and aim at some goal beyond oneself, can also nonetheless be very much about oneself—about what kind of person one is, about who one is as an individual, and about how one chooses to live one's life.[55]

The goals that underlie motivation can simultaneously be about the self and the other—they can be anchored in a person's own goals but also be about helping others.

Personal and political goals are not mutually exclusive. Having personal reasons for participating does not mean the person cannot be generally interested in politics. Similarly, having political reasons for participating does not mean the person lacks personal commitments to politics. Figure 2.1 shows that there are some people who have both, others who have neither, and some who have one but not the other. Most research has focused on people who have general commitments, regardless of whether they also have personal commitments. This book argues that without taking personal commitments into account, we overlook at least one-fifth of the population; these individuals have personal commitments but are not generally politicized. For some people, personal commitments are enough to motivate participation.

These personal goals may be more important for people from underresourced backgrounds because they are more likely to experience situations in which they lack the power to fix problems in their own lives and because they are less likely to be generally interested in politics. Lacking money, education, or societal prestige, people like Elena and Mary are more likely to lack access to health care, live in districts with underperforming public schools, or perceive injustice in their lives. These life problems have the potential to motivate people like Elena and Mary to participate in politics. Even if they do not perceive injustice in their own lives, they are more likely to know people who do, which can foster an expressive desire to fight back. In addition, they are less likely to be highly politicized, given the relationship between politicization and resources.

This approach to understanding motivation is thus distinct from past research in several key ways. First, political motivation has content. It is anchored in people's goals. Second, people's political action can emanate from their personal, not just political, concerns. Third, motivation is a process by which people choose to act, not a static trait of individuals. Motivation is constantly changing as the range of external stimuli a person perceives changes and the person's internal goals shift. Fourth, motivation necessitates constant interaction with the outside world. It emerges as individuals interact with their environments, constantly processing and prioritizing external stimuli. Unlike previous approaches that focus on the potential people have to participate, this approach outlines the process by which motivation actually emerges. Political motivation necessitates individuals making connections between their personal concerns and political action.

ISSUE PUBLICS AND MOTIVATION

Thus far, I have argued that political action can be rooted in people's personal goals. When people recognize political action as a way to fulfill important personal goals, they are moved to action. How do people make the connection between their personal concerns and political action? How do people come to recognize political action as a way of fulfilling their personal goals and concerns? Imagine, for example, a woman who generally believes that it is her civic duty to vote and believes that participation is an important part of citizenship. Life is busy, however, and she often forgets to vote on Election Day and usually does not have time for the neighborhood meetings that she regularly intends to attend. As her young children get closer to school age, she becomes concerned about the quality of education in the public schools. Ensuring the quality of education her children receive is an important personal goal for her, and she has various options for achieving it. She could make changes to the family budget to afford private school education for her children, or she could become involved in her community to improve the quality of the public schools, or she could do both. Some paths would connect her personal concerns to political action, while others would not.

When people have a deep personal commitment to an issue, they are more likely to recognize the connection between their personal goals and political action—regardless of how politicized they are. Imagine the woman in the example above. Because of her concern about her children's education, she begins to pay attention to news and information about the local schools. She sees that school board elections are approaching and informs herself about the different candidates. On that day, she makes it a point to vote and begins to be more active in the local Parent Teacher

Association as a way of getting involved in her children's education. In this example, a political issue (education) connected this woman's personal goals (improving her children's education) to politics. By paying attention to the schools, she began to get involved. She may have been generally interested in politics prior to this time, or she may not. Once politics became connected to her personal commitments, however, she made it a priority in her life.

People who connect their personal goals with a public policy issue are members of issue publics. As Nussbaum put it, this issue is "localized" for issue public members, who "ha[ve] managed to invest [the issue] with a certain importance in [their] own scheme of ends and goals."[56] Even if the policy is made in the distant halls of Congress, the issue public member has decided that the issue is of great personal concern. This personal concern can arise from a range of sources, from instrumental desires to improve the quality of a child's education to expressive desires to improve human rights for people abroad. The key is that the person has internalized that concern. Recognizing politics as a way of fulfilling personal concerns is sufficient to motivate participation for some people, regardless of how politicized they may be.

Factors other than political issues can also focus people's personal goals on political action. Research has shown that emotional advertising can elicit reactions that make people more likely to participate.[57] Negative advertisements can evoke fears and antipathies that drive people's political behavior.[58] How politicians, campaigns, and political organizations frame messages can influence whether people perceive politics as important.[59] Narratives that political elites or groups construct to define themselves can influence individuals' perceptions of the role politics plays in their lives.[60] Framing, the evocation of fear, narratives, appeals to group identity, and many other factors can help people build connections between their personal goals and political action. Issues are one of many such factors.

Issue publics represent a dynamic motivating mechanism that changes as a person's personal goals and circumstances change. The issue public hypothesis argues that regardless of how politicized people's orientations to politics are, political action is more likely when people have personal commitments to issues. Those issue commitments can emerge in a range of different ways but, importantly, they shift and change along with people's personal goals.

CONCLUSION

People have agency to choose to participate in politics. Previous models argue that people who are politically interested, efficacious, and knowledgeable have more potential for participation than those who are not similarly engaged. That is true. The trouble is that these models do not consider the conditions under which a person actually chooses to participate. Instead, they focus on the static individual traits that make it likely someone will participate. I may be more likely to participate if I am very knowledgeable about politics, but that does not necessarily mean I will choose it. When will a very knowledgeable person choose to participate? Likewise, when will someone without a lot of knowledge choose to participate? This book focuses on personal goals. As people interact with their world and prioritize stimuli for action, they choose which stimuli are in greatest need of attention. The ones most likely to get attention are those that help people meet their personal goals. People who choose to take political action do so as a way of meeting their personal goals. Studying the process allows us to examine how people make those connections instead of generalizing about what kinds of people are most likely to have made them.

The central question of this book asks how people from underresourced backgrounds become engaged in politics. I argue that issue publics are one way because issue public members are highly motivated by their personal commitments to overcome hurdles to participation. To understand how this process works, we need an understanding of motivation that shows how personal goals can be sufficient to motivate action. Previous research on political motivation was limited in this regard. This chapter thus drew on existing research in political science and psychology to outline the main characteristics of a general understanding of motivation. First, it recognizes the importance of goals in motivation. Second, it is highly personal, grounding action in people's values and personal commitments. Third, it recognizes the agency people have to choose to participate.

These characteristics of motivation lay the theoretical groundwork for understanding how membership in issue publics motivates political action. Issue public members are those who have chosen political action (made it a priority) because they see it as a way to fulfill their personal goals. As the next chapter shows, recognizing membership in issue publics as a form of political motivation broadens our sense of who can be motivated to participate in politics.

CHAPTER 3

Issue Publics and the Distribution
of Political Motivation

AMERICANS ARE NOTORIOUSLY IGNORANT about politics. A 2007 Pew Research Center study found that almost one-third of Americans could not name the vice president. Two-thirds of Americans did not know that the chief justice of the Supreme Court was politically conservative, and half of Americans could not identify Speaker of the House Nancy Pelosi. Despite extensive media coverage of his trial and eventual conviction on four counts of obstruction of justice and perjury, 71 percent of Americans did not know who Scooter Libby, former chief of staff to Vice President Dick Cheney, was.[1]

Statistics and stories like these reinforce the idea that only a small group of Americans are motivated to care about politics. These are the most politically sophisticated citizens, who are actually interested in what goes on in Washington, D.C., and take time in their lives to become informed about politics. Because they enjoy politics, they are likely to be well informed about a wide range of policy issues—from foreign policy to health care policy. This appetite for politics puts them in stark contrast to the majority of Americans who do not know the political leaning of the chief justice or cannot identify the Speaker of the House. This view of the American public, often called the attentive public model, assumes that people are political generalists: either they care about politics or they do not.

The issue public model, in contrast, assumes that people are not political generalists. Instead, people specialize and concern themselves with the issues they care most about. The concept of issue publics begins with the simple notion that in politics, different people care about different things. Some people are passionately concerned about the environment, while others may care nothing about the environment but are intensely concerned about tax policy. Still others care mostly about the state of the economy, civil rights issues, or one of a myriad of other policy issues. Many people do not care about any political issues at all. For any given issue, there is a group of people that cares about that issue and a larger group of people that does not. One person may care about both environmental policy and abortion policy, and another person may care only about abortion policy. Still another person may not care about either environmental or abortion policy but care primarily about U.S. policy toward the Middle East. People who belong to the issue public on agriculture may not know the political leanings of the Supreme Court because it is not relevant to their issue of concern. Similarly, someone who is personally concerned only about education policy may not know who Scooter Libby is, because his trial had nothing to do with education issues.

The attentive public model and the issue public model represent competing ways to think about the distribution of political motivation in the American public. Is motivation isolated to a small group of politically sophisticated elites who follow all politics? Or is motivation spread more broadly throughout the population, focused around particular issues and domains of concern? The issue public model asserts that people from a diverse range of backgrounds can care about political issues. Caring about environmental policy and being passionately concerned with tax policy do not have to be exclusively the purviews of the wealthy or the well educated. A poor person and a rich person can care personally about environmental hazards in their neighborhood, and someone with a Ph.D. and someone with only a high school education can be personally concerned about rising taxes. The issue public hypothesis thus delineates one mechanism that draws people with or without educational, financial, or civic resources into politics. If a wide range of people belong to issue publics, and if their commitments motivate issue public members to participate more in politics, a wide range of people should be motivated to participate in the political system.

Analyzing the issue public hypothesis and comparing it with the attentive public model begin with developing a richer understanding of what an issue public is and what characterizes people who belong to them. There are two key areas of inquiry. First, how realistic is the concept of issue publics? Do people really tend to choose one or two issues they especially care about? Second, do rich and poor people, the well educated and the poorly educated, belong to issue publics? Can people of all backgrounds have strong personal commitments to political issues? Examining previous research and some empirical data on issue publics allows us to answer these questions, as well as define issue publics more clearly.

WHAT ARE ISSUE PUBLICS?

Philip Converse first introduced the concept of issue publics in his seminal 1964 article, "The Nature of Belief Systems in Mass Publics." His goal was to characterize political beliefs among the mass public and, in particular, explain the "feeble" levels of coherence most members of the mass public expressed with respect to their political beliefs. He defined issue publics primarily in contrast to the mass public, most of whom

do not have meaningful beliefs, even on issues that have formed the basis for intense political controversy among elites for substantial periods of time. . . . And since it is only among "members" of any given issue public that the political effects of a controversy are felt (where such "effects" include activated public opinion expressed in the writing of letters to the editor, the changing of votes, and the like), we come a step closer to reality when we recognize the fragmentation of the mass public into a plethora of narrower issue publics.[2]

In Converse's view, issue publics consisted of the subset of people whose opinions on an issue influenced their political behavior. Most people neither changed their vote choice as the result of an issue belief nor took political action. A small subset did, however, and that subset constituted the issue public. Converse acknowledged that many people belonged to no issue publics and that some people belonged to several. The key point, in Converse's view, is that we should not view the mass public as an undifferentiated mass of voters, because members of issue publics demonstrate coherence among their belief elements that most people lack.

Subsequent scholarship extending Converse's work sought to explain why issue public members are so different from the mass public in their behavior. Jon Krosnick developed a more psychological definition of issue publics.[3] He defines issue publics as groups of people who find particular issues to be personally important. Drawing on social-psychological research, Krosnick argues that important attitudes are more likely to influence behavior because they are more accessible in memory, and individuals are more likely to become informed about issues that are important to them personally. Members of issue publics are defined by their level of attitude importance on particular issues.

In *Public Opinion and Democratic Accountability*, Vincent Hutchings broadened Converse's and Krosnick's definitions of issue publics to include not only those who actively care about a particular issue but also those who could potentially care.[4] Hutchings conceptualizes issue publics as the subset of the mass public who are potentially activated regarding a particular issue. When they do not perceive a threat to the issue, or it is not particularly salient on the political agenda, they do not pay much attention or know much about it. When something—an interest group, the media, an event—grabs their attention, however, members of the issue public can be activated.

My definition builds on this scholarship but locates the foundation of issue public membership in the motivational process. Issue public members are people who have made the connection between a political issue and their personal concerns. If motivation is a process of evaluating and prioritizing external stimuli for response, issue public members are people who have chosen attention to a political issue as a way to respond to some external stimuli. For example, Antonio is an undocumented immigrant who came to the United States with his family as a child. He and his family had not been involved in politics and did not express much general interest in politics. While he was in high school, however, he realized that his sister, who had been a strong student, would not be able to afford college because she was an undocumented immigrant and therefore would be forced to pay higher rates. He says, "The reason I got involved was because my sister—she was [a] senior and we went to the same high school—she got all of these scholarships, and then we found out she couldn't use any of them 'cause she was an undocumented immigrant. So I pretty much saw my sister's dream shattered. And also because I could see how my family was suffering because of these things."

Upon witnessing this problem in his family's life, Antonio had several options for responding. He could do nothing. He could try to find a job to help his sister find other ways to finance college. He could help his sister find alternatives to college, such as a job. Antonio chose to get involved with an advocacy organization that was fighting for immigrant rights, in particular for legislation that would give undocumented immigrants in-state tuition rates. While others may have chosen another option, Antonio saw political action as a way to solve his personal problems. As a result, he became a member of the issue public on immigrant rights. His membership in this issue public emerged as a response to an external stimuli—his sister's inability to go to college—and his desire to solve a personal problem. Like Antonio, issue public members are those who recognize politics as a way to respond to their personal concerns.

Issue public members in this definition share many of the characteristics that Converse and Krosnick identified in their research—such as coherence between belief elements, accessibility of issue concerns in memory, and likelihood of informing themselves about the issue. This definition diverges from the definition used by Hutchings, however, which includes people who have the *potential* to be activated around an issue. Although they may make the connection between their personal concerns and political issues, they have not yet done so. Hutchings's description of the way contextual factors and the political environment can shape issue concerns, however, is relevant to my understanding of how issue public membership develops and is discussed further in Chapter 5. On those topics, Hutchings's characterization of issue publics and mine converge.

A number of other concepts commonly discussed in political science are related to this concept of issue publics. In particular, extremity, constraint (the extent to which a person's beliefs are united by ideological coherence), issue salience, issue voting, and identity are several concepts that may seem to overlap. The first two—extremity and constraint—are easily distinguished from issue publics because they are characteristics of issue public members, but not the definition of them. Issue public members, in other words, are more likely to have extreme policy preferences and express constraint among their belief elements, but those characteristics do not define their membership.[5] For example, I may belong to the environmental issue public but hold relatively moderate opinions on what government should do with respect to the environment. Extreme positions are often defined by advocacy of total government control of the environment on one end of the continuum and a completely free-market approach to environmental regulation on the other. Someone who is in the environmental issue public can take a middle road between these two extreme positions but still feel strongly about the need to protect environmental resources. In a similar vein, I may be a highly educated individual who is generally very informed about political issues and expresses a great deal of constraint among my belief elements—but I may not care deeply about them. Issue public membership, in short, is defined by deep personal concern about an issue, and extremity and constraint are likely by-products of that concern.

Issue salience and issue voting are also distinct from issue public membership. These literatures do not explicitly discuss issue publics, but they do examine how varying levels of citizen concern for public policy issues affect political behavior. They have focused primarily on understanding how issue-based attitudes influence individual vote choice and candidate evaluations. Studies of issue salience and issue voting have shown that different issues are important at different times for different people, and those differences can affect people's vote choices.[6] Although homeland security was hardly an issue in the 2000 presidential election, it was a centerpiece of both parties' strategies in the 2004 election. The research on issue salience and issue voting does not ground people's issue concerns in personal levels of attitude importance, however. Although the meaning of the term "issue salience" has varied in the literature, scholars generally use it to refer to varying levels of concern for issues at any given time. Because it is defined by and measured by people's interest in an issue at one point in time, it is not clear why people have those issue-based interests. An issue may be salient, in other words, for any number of reasons that may or may not be connected to how much the person personally cares about the issue. An issue may be salient to a survey respondent because the respondent cares deeply about that issue, or because the issue has been prevalent in the media and the person has heard about it repeatedly, or because the person just happened to have a conversation with a co-worker about the issue, or because the survey itself reminded the respondent about the issue. It is easy to imagine that a person who says an issue is salient because he or she cares deeply about it will behave differently than a person who says an issue is salient because the survey instrument itself made the issue salient for the respondent. The issue public is the subset of respondents who consider an issue salient because they care personally about that issue. Because the issue is central for them, it strongly influences their political behaviors.

Identity is another related construct that is nonetheless distinct from issue public membership. Belonging to an issue public may be an important part of a person's identity but it does not define it. David Laitin defines identity as a concept that is both "primordial" and "constructed," one that is based inevitably on people's physiognomies and personal histories but also on constructed categories of membership such as race, gender, class, and personality.[7] Amy Gutmann is careful to point out that labeling these categories as social constructs does not imply that they are any more mutable than DNA or physiognomy.[8] Instead, identity recognizes that people change their ascriptive identities over time. Just as people may choose to identify with certain racial or ethnic groups, they may also choose to identify with certain issue publics. Individuals can self-identify as ardent pro-choice feminists or as strong supporters of the right to bear arms. People's identities may also inform the issue publics to which they adhere—someone who strongly identifies as Jewish is more likely to belong to the issue public on U.S. policy toward Israel. These identities are very likely to form the basis of personal concerns that people may connect to politics, but they are not themselves indications of whether someone is in an issue public.

THE ATTENTIVE PUBLIC VERSUS ISSUE PUBLICS

Conceptualizing the mass public as divided into overlapping issue publics has important implications for how we think about the distribution of political motivation in society. Existing research on issue publics is embedded in a debate about how many and what kinds of people are motivated to care about politics. In other words, how are political interest and knowledge distributed in the population? For many years, scholars have debated this question. How much do different kinds of people know and care about politics? Two distinct models have emerged to describe the distribution of political commitment in the population: the attentive public model and the issue public model. The attentive public model assumes that people are either generally motivated to pay attention to politics or not. The issue public model, in contrast, assumes people are selectively motivated: they pay attention to the issues they care most about.

Both models begin by asking what characterizes the small groups of people who are informed about and interested in politics. One of the most enduring findings in American politics is that most Americans do not care or know much about politics. Since the earliest studies of voting behavior, survey research has consistently shown that most people have little interest in politics and correspondingly lack political knowledge and information.[9] In addition, most people seem to lack a coherent political philosophy underlying their opinions, which leads to seemingly random or convoluted answers to survey questions.[10] John Zaller sums it up when he says, "Most people, on most issues, do not 'really think' any particular thing."[11] He argues that, lacking true interest in and knowledge about politics, people simply make up answers to political surveys. Their responses, then, represent nothing more than a random draw from a bag of possible policy positions and are, to use Converse's term, "non-attitudes." Among the masses of politically disengaged individuals, however, there are people with high levels of political interest and information.[12] Who are these people?

The attentive public model imagines these people as a small, sophisticated group at the top of a large mass of unsophisticated citizens. This relationship is depicted on the left side of Figure 3.1. Imagine a triangular distribution of people. At the top of the triangle is a small group of people who have high levels of political interest and thus can express real and informed political preferences on a set of issues or candidates. Gabriel Almond coined the term "attentive public" to refer to the small, elite group at the top of the triangle.[13] The majority of people lie at the bottom of the triangle and have very little, if any, political interest.

The attentive public model differentiates people by whether or not they are generally motivated to pay attention to politics. Either people are interested in everything about politics or they do not care about anything political at all. This approach assumes that people are political

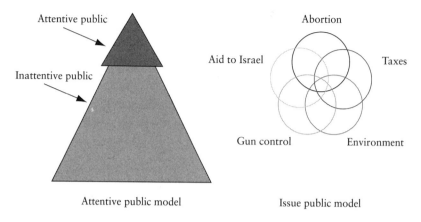

FIGURE 3.1. The attentive public and issue public models.

generalists; that is, people who are knowledgeable about one policy issue are likely to be knowledgeable about all policy issues.[14] Knowledge across issue domains does not vary; people have either high levels of information across the range of issues or low levels of information across all issues.

A growing body of research argues that people tend to be information specialists, not information generalists. People's knowledge tends to be specific to certain issue domains, and knowledge in one area does not predict knowledge in another issue area.[15] How much a person knows about abortion policy does not predict how much that person knows about economic policy. People thus tend to be most aware of political activity on particular issues. Recent research has found that policy-specific information is a better predictor of political judgments than general political knowledge[16] and that people acquire policy information in a domain-specific way.[17] Examining general levels of political knowledge, then, may not be the best way to gauge how much different people know and care about politics.

In contrast to the attentive public model, the issue public model assumes that a group of people will be engaged on each issue. Instead of having one group of elites who are informed, motivated, and engaged across all issues, there are many different people who are engaged on specific issues (as depicted on the right side of Figure 3.1).[18] The key is that people are not either engaged on all issues or unengaged in politics entirely; instead, people are most engaged on the issues they care most about. The issue public model thus presents an alternative view of the distribution of motivation in the population. People may be politically motivated even if they do not care about foreign policy. They may instead care only about civil rights issues and be motivated to be informed and active only around that issue.

As Krosnick notes, there are three premises underlying the issue public model.[19] First, most Americans give concerns such as work and family a high priority, leaving the study of politics and public affairs to compete amid a long list of secondary personal and professional priorities.[20] Second, the costs of obtaining political information are high, such that individuals must actively try if they want to be highly informed about particular policy issues.[21] And third, given limited time and energy, people will focus first on government policies they consider to be personally important. If the first two assumptions are true—that most people have personal and professional concerns that outweigh their concern for politics in general, and that the costs of obtaining political information are high—then it is not surprising that survey research has demonstrated such a persistent lack of political knowledge in the electorate. People do not know much about politics because other life concerns take priority. Because most individuals have the time and energy to be informed only about a small number of political issues, if any, they will focus on issues they consider to be most important to themselves personally.

MEASURING ISSUE PUBLICS

Assessing the validity of the issue public model depends on developing a way to measure issue publics. The key feature defining members of issue publics is personal commitment to an issue. This personal concern is distinct from thinking that an issue is important for the nation as a whole or to politics more generally. Even if I believe that it is important for the United States to figure out a sustainable long-term energy policy, it may not be an issue of great personal concern in my life. Members of issue publics are concerned with policy outcomes neither because they have a general interest in politics, nor because they think an issue is important for the nation, but because it is somehow personally important to them.

Members of the energy public, for example, would view the outcome of U.S. energy policy as being of central concern to their personal lives.

The best means of identifying who belongs to an issue public remains a matter of debate. In previous work, issue publics have been measured in four major ways: (1) inferring people's commitment to an issue from their opinions on it, (2) using demographic information to identify people who are likely to care about certain issues, (3) assessing people's commitment based on whether or not they report using issues to make political choices, and (4) directly asking people about their level of commitment to an issue. Each of these methods has drawbacks (discussed below). I use the fourth method throughout this book because it has been shown to be the best measure available.

The first method relies primarily on inferring people's level of concern based on the extremity of their opinion. This method identifies members of the issue public as either the group of people who had any opinions on a particular public policy issue or the people who had extreme opinions on it.[22] Either approach includes respondents who may not be personally committed to a particular issue. Although including people who expressed any opinion on an issue excludes survey respondents who did not offer an opinion, it may also include people who had an opinion but did not care deeply about it or people who simply fabricated a survey response. Including only those with an extreme opinion is more refined than simply including all who responded with an opinion, but it still does not directly assess a citizen's level of personal concern. Instead, it conflates extremity with passion. It assumes that all respondents with extreme opinions care deeply about those opinions. Although some research has shown that extreme opinions are often personally important, it is not clear that all personally important opinions are extreme.[23] A wealthy liberal who believes in welfare may have an extreme opinion on the level of government services that should be offered to the poor without having a personal stake in that opinion. Similarly, it is easy to imagine a person who has an extreme opinion on Middle East policy or stem cell research without feeling that it is an issue of particular personal concern to them. American National Election Studies (ANES) data from 1996 shows that on issues related to government services, only 24 percent of individuals with personal commitments take an extreme position. Even on an issue like abortion, where we would expect more extremism among people who care about the issue, ANES data shows that in 1996 almost 40 percent of respondents with strong personal commitments to abortion issues did not have extreme preferences.

The second method that researchers have used to measure personal political commitments is to rely on people's demographic characteristics. For example, researchers assume that all parents with school-age children are personally concerned about education policy, that all African-Americans are personally concerned about civil rights issues, and that all regular churchgoers are personally concerned about abortion.[24] The advantage of this method is that it does not rely on self-reported data. Instead, it uses observable characteristics of the individual to evaluate whether or not that person is likely to be committed. This measure is also somewhat crude, however, because it assumes a perfect correlation between demographic characteristics and political beliefs. Undoubtedly, some regular churchgoers are not engaged in the political agenda of the church. Likewise, parents (such as those with children in private schools) are not always engaged in education policy in their communities.

The third approach indirectly assesses people's personal commitments to political issues by examining the reasons they give for evaluating candidates and parties. It draws on open-ended survey questions that ask citizens what they like and dislike about political candidates and parties, assuming that individuals who ground their evaluations in specific issues have personal concern for those issues.[25] The advantage of this approach is that it mitigates potential problems with self-reported measures such as social desirability, whereby respondents feel pressured to say that they care personally about an issue even if they do not. If social desirability bias were a problem, then self-report questions should yield higher numbers of respondents who purportedly care personally about an issue than do these open-ended questions. The two methods, however, yield similar results in terms of the proportion of the population with political commitments and relationships between motivation and political knowledge.[26] It is thus unclear that this third approach offers much advantage over the alternatives. In addition, a weakness of the open-ended question approach is that it provides a less consistent set of responses about which issues individuals care about.[27]

The fourth approach, and the one used in this book, relies on closed-ended survey questions that directly ask respondents how much they personally care about an issue. These questions have the advantage of directly probing respondents' level of personal concern. As a result, previous research has found that it generates a more refined measure and yields a more consistent set of data than other approaches.[28] Operationally, this means that I measure issue publics by drawing on survey questions that directly ask respondents how personally important issues are to them. The issue public is the subset of citizens who say that a particular issue is personally extremely important or is one of the most important issues to them.[29]

In this chapter, I draw primarily on ANES data from 1980, 1984, 1996, 2000, and 2004 because those are the years in which the ANES asked respondents to identify their positions on a range of issues, as well as their level of personal concern about them. Although the questions varied slightly from year to year, the ANES generally asked people to identify their opinions on a seven-point scale and then asked them how personally important the issue was to them.[30] For example, in 1996 the ANES asked respondents for their opinions on five issues: defense spending, government aid to minorities, abortion, the trade-off between environmental protection and jobs, and the trade-off between government services and spending. After ascertaining an individual's opinion, the ANES then asked about the importance of the issue. The specific question read, "How important is this issue to YOU?" Instead of asking people how important defense spending is for the nation or how important environmental protection is for all people, the question asked how important the issues were to respondents themselves. I may think that military security is important for the nation as a whole, but I may not feel that it is personally important in my life. Respondents could respond "extremely important," "very important," "somewhat important," "not too important," or "not important at all." Consistent with previous research, I coded anyone who said that at least one issue was "extremely important" as belonging to an issue public.[31]

One limitation of this measure relative to broader specifications of political motivation is that it is centered on people's personal concerns about particular political issues. However, people's personal concerns may or may not be about issues (they could instead be about things like the level of polarization in politics, the degree of political corruption, or the role of the Electoral College). This measure is still an improvement over generalized measures of political interest, knowledge, and efficacy, which are all content-free.[32] Studies of the substance of people's political commitments have found that they are most likely to state issue-oriented commitments.[33] In addition, content-based measures are consistent with the premise that being in an issue public is about connecting people's personal concerns to political issues through emotions. If I feel angry, I am angry about something particular, instead of being angry in the abstract.[34] Likewise, people's personal concerns have targets. I am not concerned about politics in the abstract—instead, I am concerned about something particular, whether it is the environment, taxes, or the level of civility in political discourse. Thus, although this measure does not encompass the full range of things people can care passionately about in politics, it does capture a key subset of things people are likely to care about—policy outcomes. As the best available measure of issue publics, it allows us to develop a fuller understanding of the characteristics of issue publics and issue public members.

DO PEOPLE SPECIALIZE?

Assessing the issue public model necessitates asking whether or not people specialize in the issues they care about. An examination of the numbers and kinds of personal commitments people have in politics demonstrates that people do have specialized political commitments. People are not motivated to care about politics broadly; they are motivated about particular issues and areas of personal concern. Figure 3.2 examines the number of personal political commitments people have. Drawing on ANES data in 1980, 1984, 1996, 2000, and 2004 cross-sectional studies, the graph shows the percentage of respondents who have zero, one, two, or more than two personal commitments.[35] Obviously, the proportion of people who express at least one strong policy commitment is dependent on the number of issues the survey asks about. In 1980, 41.5 percent of respondents are passionately committed to at least one of eight issues; in 1984, 37.2 percent of respondents are committed to at least one of four issues; in 1996, 60.1 percent

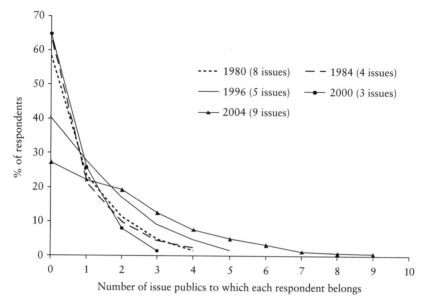

FIGURE 3.2. Percentages of respondents with varying numbers of personal commitments. SOURCE: Data from the 1980, 1984, 1996, 2000, and 2004 ANES cross-sectional studies.

of respondents are committed to at least one of five issues; and in 2000, 35.3 percent of respondents are committed to at least one of three issues. The 2004 study yielded the highest percentage of respondents committed to at least one issue (72 percent), but it asked about nine issues, all of which were highly salient to that election.

The key point is that many people in these data are specialists, not generalists. They appear to direct their personal concern toward specific issues, rather than focusing on politics more generally. Although approximately a quarter of all respondents in each cross-sectional study are committed to at least one issue, the number of people professing strong commitment to more than one issue is dramatically lower. With the exception of 1996 and 2004, the percentage of people who are committed to two issues is less than half the percentage of people committed to just one. In 1996 and 2004, the percentage of people committed to more than two issues is less than half the percentage of people committed to just one. In addition, if respondents in 1996 or 2004 were very committed to more than one issue, the issues were often related. For example, 51 percent of respondents who cared personally about abortion also had a strong personal commitment to women's equality. If people were not specialists, then we would expect people who were committed to one issue to be committed to many issues. What if enthusiastic survey respondents said that every issue was extremely important to them while more dour respondents said none was important to them? Then we would expect that people had either no issue commitments or multiple commitments. Instead, people are most likely to be committed to one of the issues studied in the ANES or none of them.

Another question is what percentage of the population personally cares about each issue? Figure 3.3 graphs the percentage of respondents who have strong personal commitments to each issue. Clearly, variation exists across the different issues. From 1980 to 2004, approximately

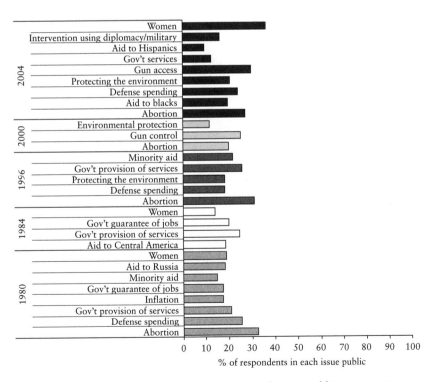

FIGURE 3.3. Percentages of respondents in each issue public. SOURCE: Data from the 1980, 1984, 1996, 2000, and 2004 ANES cross-sectional studies.

15 to 30 percent of respondents are highly committed to each issue. Abortion has the largest group of motivated adherents in both 1980 and 1996. The group of people who are passionately committed to abortion issues is 5 percentage points larger than the second-largest group in each year, which is indicative of the unusually large size of the abortion public. The average group size seems to be around 20 percent, or one-fifth, of all respondents. The issues included in this analysis are those that figured prominently in the election of the given year. The ANES chose issues that were a large part of the campaign dialogue. Thus it is possible—and, in fact, quite probable—that there are many more issues for which the group of people with passionate commitments is much smaller than one-fifth of the population. For instance, if the ANES asked respondents how much they cared personally about space policy, it is difficult to imagine that 20 percent of all respondents would say that space policy is extremely important to them personally.

These data indicate that many people are political specialists. People are likely to care passionately about one or two political issues, instead of politics writ large. Insofar as caring personally about a policy issue is a form of political motivation, it appears that motivation is not isolated to a small "attentive public." The sheer numbers of people who have personal commitments to policy issues indicate that motivation is not isolated to a small group of elites.

WHAT IS THE RELATIONSHIP BETWEEN ISSUE PUBLICS AND GENERAL INDICATORS OF MOTIVATION?

Previous research has shown that issue public members exhibit political behaviors that are commonly associated with political elites. Research in psychology shows that highly important attitudes are more likely to affect people's decision-making processes and more likely to affect their behaviors.[36] In part, this is because attitudes that are personally important are more accessible in people's memories,[37] and people are more likely to be motivated to inform themselves about political activity related to that attitude. Logically, it is easy to see why this might be true: most people are too busy and find it too difficult to concern themselves with the bewildering array of ongoing policy debates. In order to become informed about a particular policy issue, the individual must be highly motivated. Individuals are most likely to be motivated to inform themselves about issues that they think matter most in their lives.

Issue public members are also behaviorally different from the broader electorate with respect to their specific issue.[38] As findings from psychology show, attitudes within issue publics are highly accessible in memory, resistant to change, highly stable over time, and linked to individuals' basic values.[39] In addition, attitudes within issue publics are anchored by issue-specific policy knowledge that informs the individuals' political choices.[40] Members of issue publics are more likely to know about candidates' political stands and more likely to perceive differences between competing candidates on issues of personal concern to them. Members of issue publics are information specialists whose specialized knowledge may not be apparent in surveys measuring only generalized levels of political knowledge. Unlike voters in the general electorate who do not care about a particular issue, members of issue publics are motivated by their high levels of personal concern to behave differently than most individuals. They have more stable preferences regarding the issue they care about, and those preferences are more likely to affect their voting behavior.

These findings on the impact that high personal concern for an issue can have on people's behavior buttresses the issue public model. Personal concern differentiates members of issue publics from the public at large because it motivates them to become more informed and more knowledgeable about their issue of concern. Members of the abortion public are informed about abortion issues but may be largely uninformed about other political issues and may do poorly on tests of general political knowledge. Similarly, members of the issue public on farm policy may be very knowledgeable about agricultural issues, even if they are not generally politically sophisticated.

Does this mean that issue publics are simply another way of describing people who are politicized? It is possible that belonging to an issue public can spark people to become more interested in and aware of politics—or that people who are generally interested and aware about politics will be more likely to be in issue publics. If either (or both) of these possibilities is true, then issue public members should have higher levels of general political motivation than non–issue public members. In Figure 2.1, however, the percentage of issue public members who have less politicized orientations is comparable to the percentage of highly politicized orientations. Further, Figure 3.4 graphs the average levels of political interest, knowledge, and efficacy, as well as partisanship, for issue public members and non–issue public members in the 1996 ANES. Previous research has shown that political elites rank much higher than the general population on these measures of political motivation.[41] The graph shows, however, that issue public members are only slightly more interested in politics and slightly more partisan than non–issue public members, and the groups are virtually indistinguishable on measures of political knowledge and efficacy. Belonging to an issue public has important ramifications for people's attitudes and behaviors with respect to their issue of concern, but it does not necessarily affect overall levels of political orientation. They may be slightly more interested in politics and slightly more partisan than non–issue public members, but they are no more likely to know more about politics or feel like they have more say in government.

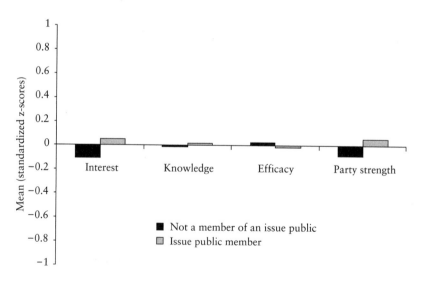

FIGURE 3.4. Mean levels of political interest, knowledge, efficacy, and party strength among issue public members and nonmembers. SOURCE: Data from the 1996 ANES cross-sectional study.

ARE ISSUE PUBLIC MEMBERS POLITICAL ELITES?

The attentive public and issue public models also make different predictions about what kinds of people are motivated to care about politics. The attentive public model predicts a relatively small group of elites will be motivated. The issue public model, in contrast, predicts that political motivation is not necessarily restricted to a small group of elites, because many different kinds of people can care about many different issues.

An examination of income differences between people who are and people who are not motivated to participate in politics demonstrates that motivation is not isolated to a narrow wealthy elite. Figure 3.5 graphs the average difference in income between the two groups of respondents. The graph shows two different ways of assessing motivation: The first examines whether or not people have personal policy commitments. The second uses a generalized measure of political interest. People with high political interest are much more likely to be wealthy than people with low political interest.[42] The disparities in income between people with high and low levels of generalized political interest are much greater than the disparities

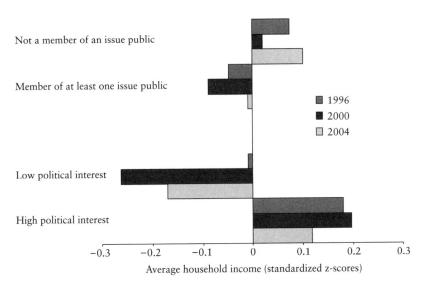

FIGURE 3.5. Average household income for respondents at varying levels of political motivation. SOURCE: Data from the 1996, 2000, and 2004 ANES cross-sectional studies.

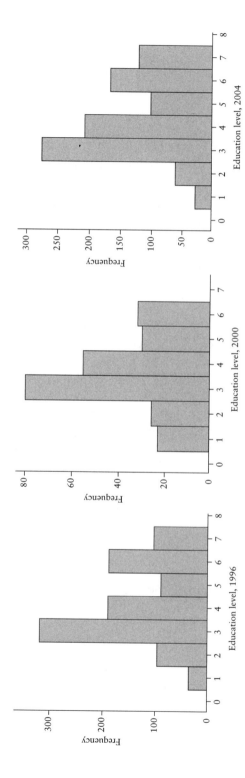

FIGURE 3.6. Distribution of education among issue public members. SOURCE: Data from the 1996, 2000, and 2004 ANES cross-sectional studies.

between people who do and do not belong to issue publics. Although not shown here, a parallel graph for education would display the same pattern: differences in educational attainment for people with high and low levels of political interest are much larger than differences between issue public members and non–issue public members.

Figure 3.5 shows that, overall, issue public members are likely to have slightly lower incomes than people who are not issue public members. The disparities do differ by issue, however. If we examine the five issues studied in the 1996 ANES, for example, we see that there are some issues for which issue public members are statistically indistinguishable from non–issue public members in terms of income. On issues related to the provision of government services and the environment, issue public members are statistically no different from non–issue public members in average income level. On issues related to defense and minority aid, however, issue public members have slightly lower incomes than non–issue public members, and the differences are statistically significant. Members of the abortion public have slightly higher incomes than non–issue public members. Issues vary, in other words, in what kinds of adherents they attract. There is no clear pattern, however, whereby issue public members are always poorer or richer than non–issue public members. Issue publics are thus different from other indicators of political motivation, like general political interest. Although being generally interested in politics is always associated with higher income, being in an issue public is not.

Our conception of how broadly political motivation is distributed in the population depends on how we conceptualize motivation. If we think political motivation is purely a function of indicators like generalized political interest, then it appears that wealthy people are much more likely to be motivated to participate than poorer people. But if we take seriously the role of personal policy commitments in motivating political action, then it becomes clear that the income differences between people who are and are not motivated are not nearly as stark.

Similar patterns emerge when we examine education. Figure 3.6 shows that people at all levels of education have personal commitments to political issues. This figure shows the distribution of education among people who belong to an issue public in the 1996, 2000, and 2004 ANES data.

Membership in an issue public is clearly not restricted to people of high education; people at all educational levels demonstrate strong personal commitments to political issues.

The key point is that people of many backgrounds care personally about political issues. This makes sense, as parents from many different backgrounds can care passionately about education policy if it affects their children. Similarly, people at many income levels may care personally about abortion policy, especially if their church advocates a particular position. Conceptualizing motivation in this way reveals that a range of different kinds of people can be motivated to participate in politics. The issue public model thus allows for a broader distribution of political motivation in the population than the attentive public model. People do not have to be generally interested in politics to care about the schools their children attend or the health care their parents receive. People of all backgrounds can have personal concern about an issue and belong to issue publics.

CONCLUDING THOUGHTS

The issue public model begins with the simple notion that different people care about different things. Taking this idea seriously, the issue public model incorporates differing levels of personal concern about policy issues into our understanding of the distribution of political interest, information, and knowledge among the public. Instead of thinking of the mass public as generalists, the issue public model thinks about them as specialists, subdivided into issue publics based on the issues they care most about personally. In looking empirically at issue publics, we find that people do differentiate their levels of passion about particular issues and that they tend to be passionate about a limited number of discrete issues, if any.

The data in this chapter also show that belonging to an issue public is not restricted to people of greater education, income, or other political and civic resources. Even if people of higher educational and financial backgrounds may be more likely to belong to issue publics, the fact that people without much education or money can belong to issue publics is significant. People without much education or money may be motivated by their personal concern for particular issues to behave as other members of the issue public—to be more informed, knowledgeable, and active on their issue of concern. This lays the foundation for the next questions: Does belonging to an issue public motivate people to participate in politics? In particular, does it help draw people of disadvantaged backgrounds into the political system? Exploring these questions reveals the implications that issue publics have for the functioning of the democratic system.

CHAPTER 4

An Empirical Look at Issue
Publics and Participation

THROUGHOUT AMERICAN HISTORY, there are striking examples of
disadvantaged minorities rising up to fight for their political rights. These
examples reveal mechanisms that can draw traditionally marginalized
individuals into the political system. One of the most striking examples
is the Montgomery Bus Boycott, which marked the beginning of the civil
rights movement in 1955. In this and other revolutionary moments in
American history, masses of marginalized individuals endured considerable hardship to fight for their rights.

As for the boycotters themselves, the religious fervor they went to bed with
at night always congealed by the next morning into cold practicality, as they
faced rainstorms, mechanical breakdowns, stranded relatives, and complicated
relays in getting from home to job without being late or getting fired or getting into an argument with the employer, then getting home again, perhaps
having to find a way to and from the grocery store, and cooking and eating
supper, dealing with children and housework, then perhaps going back out
into the night for a mass meeting and finally home again, recharged by the
"rousements" of [Reverend Ralph] Abernathy and the inspiration of [Rever-
end Martin Luther] King, and then at last some weary but contented sleep
before the aching chill of dawn started the cycle all over again. To a largely
uneducated people among whom the most common occupations were maid
and day laborer, the loss of what was for many their most important modern
convenience—cheap bus transportation—left them with staggering problems
of logistics and morale. . . . [Nonetheless,] between 30,000 and 40,000 Negro
fares were being denied to the buses every day.[1]

Despite extreme challenges, including managing daily life without transportation, thousands of poor, uneducated African-Americans found the
motivation to sustain the boycott for 381 days. In doing so, they defied
models of political participation that view minorities and people with low

levels of education and income as unlikely to participate in the political system.[2] Not only did these individuals participate, but they did so at considerable economic and personal cost to themselves.

Motivation was a key factor in the ability of protestors in Montgomery to sustain the bus boycott. All of the protestors were personally affected by the segregation laws they were trying to defeat. Their participation had a specific goal that, if achieved, would have a direct impact on their lives. These personal commitments, combined with the support and strength that arose from the collective experience, motivated them to participate in new ways in the political system. Their motivation was strong enough to overcome the costs associated with participation. The Montgomery Bus Boycott is an extreme example of people participating in politics when the personal cost was very high. In many other instances that are not captured by history books, traditionally marginalized individuals have taken part in the political system against all odds because they were highly motivated to do so.

This chapter empirically examines how personal issue commitments affect participation. Instead of focusing on the demographic characteristics or personal resources that facilitate participation, the issue public hypothesis examines the underlying desires people have to participate in politics (or not). In particular, this hypothesis argues that people's reasons for participating in politics can be rooted in their personal commitments to particular issues. Demonstrating the effect of issue publics on participation entails answering two questions: First, does belonging to an issue public facilitate participation? Second, is this type of motivation particularly important for people who, like the boycotters, lack educational, financial, and civic resources? The analyses in this chapter thus test two hypotheses: first, that personal issue commitments can motivate participation and, second, that these commitments have a larger effect on participation for underresourced individuals. Incorporating the notion of issue publics into models of participation helps us better understand participation among citizens who do not have many participatory resources. By showing that people who are personally committed to political issues will be more likely to take action, this chapter reveals a key mechanism for incorporating people with fewer financial, educational, and civic resources into the political system.

ISSUE PUBLICS AND PARTICIPATION

Unlike existing models that have no sense of the goals people are trying to achieve through participation, the issue public hypothesis recognizes the importance of personal policy commitments. Instead of focusing on the political orientations that are most prevalent among citizens with financial, educational, and civic resources, the issue public hypothesis focuses on personal commitments to issues, which are a source of motivation that people of all backgrounds can have. Even if people are not generally politically aware or sophisticated, they can still be motivated to participate. Focusing on the specific commitments that motivate action thus enables the issue public hypothesis to explain the participation of the Montgomery Bus Boycotters while traditional models of participation cannot. If we assessed their motivation by looking only at general levels of political interest, the Montgomery Bus Boycotters may not have appeared to be very motivated. Yet, they overcame great barriers to participation. The issue public hypothesis explains this by examining the strong personal commitment they had to ending segregation. This commitment motivated people without much money, education, or high levels of general interest in politics to make great sacrifices to participate.

Some previous research suggests that personal policy commitments can be important motivators of participation. Several classic studies of political participation, such as Campbell, Converse, Miller, and Stokes's *The American Voter*, Wolfinger and Rosenstone's *Who Votes?* and Verba, Schlozman, and Brady's *Voice and Equality*, have found that individuals who have a personal stake in government policy are more likely to participate than individuals who do not.[3] These studies, however, have been hampered by indirect measures of personal commitment or issue-specific data that prevent generalization about the impact of personal commitments on participation.[4] M. Kent Jennings and Ellen Ann Andersen reinforce findings about the relationship between personal commitments and participation, finding that the personal desire to affect AIDS policy can be an important motivator of AIDS activism.[5] Similarly, Penny Visser, Jon Krosnick, and Joseph Simmons examine voting and persuasion and find that individuals whose political attitudes are more personally central are more likely to vote and persuade others politically.[6] Although these studies indicate that an exploration of personalized political motivations to participate is needed, the topic has not yet been systematically analyzed. Past studies were domain-specific or looked only at activists,[7] at specific issue areas,[8] or at particular kinds of participation.[9] Further, none of these studies looked at whether the impact of issue public membership varies with individual resources.

Simple bivariate data presented in Chapter 2 (see Figure 2.1) shows that, on average, issue public members participate at higher rates than nonmembers and that the gap between the two groups is larger for respondents with low levels of politicized orientations than respondents with high levels. Figure 4.1 looks more directly at the impact of educational resources, by graphing the difference in rates of participation between issue public members and nonmembers at three education levels. The graph uses a summary scale of participation in eight activities (described further in Appendix B). The activities are as follows (the percentage of respondents

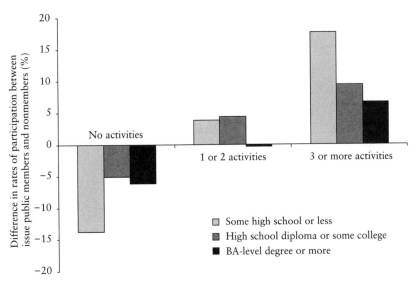

FIGURE 4.1. Difference in rates of participation between issue public members and nonmembers, conditional on educational attainment. Bars represent the difference in the percentages of members and nonmembers at each education level. Participation rates are based on a summary scale of participation in eight activities (described further in the text and in Appendix B). SOURCE: Data from the 1996 ANES cross-sectional study.

who reported engaging at some level in each type of activity is reported in parentheses): (1) voting in the 1996 election (77 percent), (2) spending time volunteering in the past year (42 percent), (3) being involved with a group in which the respondent discusses politics (38 percent), (4) talking to others to persuade them to vote for or against a party or candidate (29 percent), (5) working with others or joining an organization to work on a community problem (23 percent), (6) attending meetings, speeches, or rallies for a candidate (6 percent), (7) contributing money to a political candidate or cause (6 percent), and (8) working for any one of the parties or candidates (3 percent). Overall, 12 percent of respondents in the 1996 ANES engaged in no activities, 25 percent engaged in only one activity, and 24 percent engaged in two activities (the most popular were voting and doing volunteer work). Twenty percent of respondents reported engaging in three activities, and 19 percent or fewer engaged in four, five, six, seven, or eight activities.

Putting differences in education aside for a moment, the descriptive data show that, overall, people who belong to issue publics are more likely to participate in politics than those who do not. In Figure 4.1 the difference between issue public members and nonmembers (at virtually all educational levels) is positive for participation in one or more activities, meaning that issue public members participate at higher rates than nonmembers. The difference is negative for those participating in no activities, indicating that nonmembers of any education level are more likely not to participate in any activities. Overall, only 9 percent of issue public members participated in no activities, while 16 percent of nonmembers participated in no activities.

Figure 4.1 divides the respondents into three groups based on their education level and shows that the differences in participation between issue public members and nonmembers are greatest among people with less education, with nonmembers less likely to participate overall. Non–issue public members who have less than a high school degree are 14 percentage points more likely than their member counterparts to participate in no activities. The difference between issue public members and nonmembers who have a bachelor's degree or more and participate in no activities is 6 percentage points. Likewise, among respondents who have no high school diploma, issue public members are almost 18 percentage points more likely to participate in three or more activities than nonmembers. Among respondents who have at least a bachelors' degree, the difference between the two groups is only 7 percentage points. Issue public members are always more likely to participate than nonmembers, but the differences are particularly stark among people with less education. Belonging to an issue public appears to have a stronger effect on participation among people with less education.

These initial studies and basic descriptive analyses lay the foundation for further multivariate analysis. What if belonging to an issue public is merely a proxy for something else? For example, people with higher socioeconomic status might be more likely to report belonging to an issue public since they are more likely to have the networks, information, and knowledge necessary to connect politics to their personal concerns. Unless we take socioeconomic status into account, any relationship we observe between issue publics and participation could be an artifact of the well-known relationship between socioeconomic status and participation. To account for this and other potential confounds, we need to conduct a full regression analysis of the relationship between resources, issue public membership, and participation. Regression analyses in this chapter thus begin by examining the relationship between issue publics and participation and subsequently examine whether issue public membership has a stronger effect among people with fewer resources for participation.

DESCRIBING THE DATA

Conducting a regression analysis of the relationship between issue publics and political participation presents two main empirical challenges. The first is finding good measures of issue public membership, as discussed in the previous chapter. The second is determining causality: How do we know that belonging to an issue public causes people to become more politically involved, as opposed to political involvement causing people to become committed to an issue? These are complicated issues to untangle, and perfect data to address them do not exist. I draw on two datasets with different strengths and weaknesses to show that issue publics do affect participation, even if we measure the effect in several ways.

The two datasets used in the analysis have complementary strengths and weaknesses relative to the empirical challenges outlined above. The first dataset is the 1996 American National Election Study (ANES). It has strong measures of issue public membership and includes measures of other variables necessary to analyze political participation. The drawback is that it does not provide much help in addressing issues of causality. A common approach to handling issues of causality in observational data is to use instrumental variables. The 1996 ANES, however, does not provide good instruments for issue public membership. The second dataset is the 1990 American Citizen Participation Study (CPS). This dataset provides less refined and less direct measures of issue public membership but contains better data for addressing issues of causality. Unlike the 1996 ANES, this dataset has good variables that can be used to measure issue public membership. Given their contrasting strengths and weaknesses, both datasets are used throughout all of the analyses.

The basic regression model builds on the civic voluntarism model used in Verba, Schlozman, and Brady's *Voice and Equality* because it is often considered the clearest expression of the dominant resource-mobilization model.[10] Building this model raises questions about measuring intangible concepts like motivation and modeling the relationship between these variables. I briefly deal with some of those questions here. (See Appendix B for more detail and a comparison of the specific measures used from each dataset.)

The first question is how to measure the dependent variable, political participation. To reflect the range of ways in which people participate in politics, I develop one measure that captures respondents' overall levels of political activity. This measure includes four types of activities (voting, contributing money, participating in activities that require individuals to expend considerable amounts of time, and engaging in political discussion). The overall activity scale in the 1996 ANES is constructed as specified above in the discussion of Figure 4.1. The overall activity scale in the 1990 CPS was constructed similarly. It is an additive scale of the following activities: working on a campaign, contributing campaign money, joining a political organization, writing a letter to an official, trying to persuade someone how to vote, and attending a political meeting or rally. A respondent received one point for each activity in which she participated. On average, respondents participated in 2.5 activities, but the modal number of activities was one.

The primary predictor of participation I examine is personal commitment to an issue. As noted in Chapter 3, the 1996 ANES asked respondents about their opinions on five issues: defense spending, government aid to minorities, abortion, the trade-off between environmental protection and jobs, and the trade-off between government services and spending. The ANES then asked them: "How important is this issue to YOU?" Respondents could choose one of five responses: 1, extremely important; 2, very important; 3, somewhat important; 4, not too important; 5, not important at all. Consistent with work by Krosnick, and as discussed in Chapter 3, the issue public is defined as the subset of people who responded that the issue was "extremely important" to them.

Identifying issue public members in the American Citizen Participation Study was more complicated. This study did not ask respondents whether they had personal commitments to specific issues but instead asked the extent to which their participation was driven by commitment to an issue. The specific question read: "Thinking about your activity [insert type of activity], were there any issues or problems ranging from public policy issues to community, family, or personal concerns that led you to become active in [insert type of activity]?" If people responded yes, they were asked to name the specific issue in an open-ended question. Then another question, designed to see who was affected by the problem, followed: "Thinking about the (first) issue you mentioned, that is [insert issue named], which of these categories best describes who was affected by the problem?" Respondents could choose one of these answers: (a) only myself or my family, (b) only other people, but not myself or my family, (c) myself or my family, as well as others like us, (d) all people in the community, (e) all people in the nation or all people in the world. I identified as issue public members those who named a specific issue that drove their involvement in politics, excluding those who said the issue affected "only other people, but not myself or my family." All other response categories were consistent with the idea that issue public membership is rooted in issues that subjects view as personally important. With the exception of the option of saying that the issue was important only for others, the remaining response categories can be viewed as a series of concentric circles. Issues that affect only the respondent or the respondent's family are in the middle, with issues that affect "all people in the nation or all people in the world" in the largest circle. Even the largest circle includes the respondent in the middle. Among those participating in one activity, 49 percent of the respondents reported having a personal issue commitment. The measure used in the analysis was the ratio of the number of activities the person said were driven by personal concern about an issue to the total number of activities in which the respondent participated. This ratio ranged from zero to one, with a mean of .48, indicating that slightly less than half of the mean respondent's participation was driven by issue commitments.

How do we know that issue public membership has a causal effect on participation? The relationship between issue publics and participation is likely a two-way street. The hypothesis being tested here is that having greater personal commitment to a political issue, regardless of how that commitment originates, can spur greater participation in activities relating to it. At the same time, people's commitment to issues is likely to deepen as they become more involved and more invested in the work and come into closer contact with other people who share their commitments (discussed in Chapter 5). People who become active in the National Rifle Association, for example, could become more committed to gun rights as they engage in more discussions with people who feel strongly about Second Amendment rights and spend more time working on related issues.

Thus the key independent variable, issue public membership, might be both the cause and the result of the dependent variable, political participation. Given the possibility of a reciprocal relationship, we need techniques that allow us to disentangle the complicated relationship. Instrumental variables and two-stage least-squares regression are commonly used techniques. An advantage of the CPS is that it included variables that can be used as effective instruments for issue public membership. Instrumental variables are variables correlated with membership in an issue public (the independent variable) but not caused by political participation (the dependent variable). To identify instruments for issue public membership, I use a logic that mirrors that used by Verba, Schlozman, and Brady.[11] The instruments used in my analysis were as follows: being a victim of gender, racial, or religious bias; having material dependence on government (such as welfare or Social Security); having problems (such as limited access to health care or high-quality education) that government can solve; religious attendance; job prestige; participation in nonpolitical organizations; participation in high school government; and political socialization. The first set of instruments—being a victim of sexual, racial, or religious bias; having material dependence on government; and having problems that government can solve—consists of variables caused by exogenous factors. The factors that cause victimization by prejudice or produce problems that government can solve are most likely distinct from the factors that predict participation. Similarly, consistent with arguments made by Verba, Schlozman, and Brady, I assume that people are unlikely to choose their job, join a nonpolitical organization, or attend church as a result of their political participation. Lastly, participation in high school government and political socialization are included as instruments because they are temporally prior to the dependent variable, participation, and therefore cannot have been caused by it.

Both models also include traditional measures of political motivation to see if issue public membership has any independent effect on participation. Traditionally, researchers have measured political motivation by assessing the extent to which an individual pays attention to and follows politics (political interest), has taken the time to inform herself about it (political knowledge), and feels like her actions matter (political efficacy). Scholars have sometimes included strength of party identification as a measure of political motivation, since people who identify as strong Republicans or strong Democrats are generally quite engaged in politics.[12] This study includes measures of the respondent's score on the political interest, efficacy, and knowledge scales. A separate variable measures partisan strength. Together these measures capture the individual's overall level of politicization and the degree to which she has psychological attachments to politics.

Also included in the model are a series of independent variables that capture the effect of resources and recruitment. As in the civic voluntarism model, resources and recruitment are conceptualized as a set of material and nonmaterial resources that individuals accrue through their institutional affiliations. Several resources and recruitment measures are incorporated in the model. First, the model includes measures of socioeconomic status. Whether socioeconomic status affects participation because it makes individuals more likely to be a part of institutions that endow them with participatory resources[13] or because it places individuals at the center of important social and political networks,[14] socioeconomic status is an important predictor of political activity. Here it is measured using two variables: the respondent's level of education and the respondent's family income. The CPS model additionally includes the respondent's score on a vocabulary test as a measure of educational resources.

Second, both models include measures of civic skills. A central component of the civic voluntarism model is the set of civic skills that individuals develop through their institutional affiliations. Individuals who have the skills required for participation are more likely to participate. The CPS identifies three domains in which individuals may practice civic skills: job, organizations, and church. For each domain, respondents are asked if they had written a letter, gone to a meeting where they took part in making decisions, planned or chaired a meeting, or gave a presentation or speech. Responses are added to create a total measure of civic skills. Although the 1996 ANES does not specifically ask individuals what skills they practice through their various institutional affiliations, it does ask them whether they have taken part in the activities of nineteen types of voluntary associations. Verba, Schlozman, and Brady find that membership in these types of associations increases civic skills.[15] Thus, civic skills are measured as the number of organizations in which the respondent has taken part in group activities.

Third, the model includes measures of recruitment. In addition to all the resources an individual accrues through her institutional affiliations, she can also be mobilized through them. The 1996 ANES asks respondents whether they were contacted by a variety of types of organizations about the campaign: political parties, religious or moral groups, or any other groups. Recruitment is measured using an additive scale based on the number of different types of groups that contacted the respondent. The 1990 CPS asks respondents whether they were recruited for participation for specific types of activity. The recruitment variable in this dataset is measured as the sum of whether or not the respondent was asked to contact a government official, take part in a protest, or take part in local community work, and the number of times the respondent was asked to work for or contribute to a campaign or candidate.

Finally, a set of standard demographic variables is included in the model. Dichotomous variables are included for the following: (1) whether or not the respondent's parents were both born in the United States, (2) whether or not the respondent is presently working, (3) whether or not the respondent is retired, and (4) whether or not the respondent is Catholic. Variables for the respondent's age are also included.

HYPOTHESIS 1:
PERSONAL ISSUE COMMITMENTS
CAN MOTIVATE PARTICIPATION

The first hypothesis asks what effect, if any, personal issue commitments have on participation. The analysis in Table 4.1 shows the results for both models, using data from the 1996 ANES and the 1990 CPS. Across both datasets and model specifications, having personal issue commitments has a statistically significant and positive impact on a person's decision to participate even after factors commonly thought to explain participation—resources, recruitment, and general levels of engagement—are taken into account. With respect to resources, recruitment, and indicators of general interest in politics, the results of both models are largely consistent with previous studies of participation. People with more education, income, and civic skills are statistically more likely to participate in more activities. People who are recruited are more likely to participate. Not surprisingly, the analysis also shows that people with stronger psychological orientations toward politics are more likely to participate. This makes sense. People who take the time in their day-to-day lives to follow politics and inform themselves about it will naturally be more likely to take the time to participate than people who do not make politics a part of their daily lives.

This analysis is distinct from previous models of participation because it includes measures of personal issue commitments. The results show that having these personal issue commitments affects participation above and beyond the effects of resources, recruitment, and general

TABLE 4.1. Regression of overall activity on personal issue commitments and other predictors of participation

	1996 American National Elections Study			1990 American Citizen Participation Study		
	B	Std. error		B	Std. error	
Motivation						
Issue commitments[a]	0.088	(0.036)	**	1.413	(0.138)	†
Party strength	0.042	(0.023)	*	0.159	(0.038)	†
Political interest	0.188	(0.031)	†	0.211	(0.027)	†
Political knowledge	0.038	(0.024)		0.065	(0.021)	***
Political efficacy	−0.004	(0.016)		0.071	(0.015)	†
Resources						
Education	0.048	(0.012)	†	0.071	(0.034)	**
Vocabulary				−0.030	(0.019)	
Household income	0.049	(0.013)	†	0.016	(0.027)	
Free time				0.007	(0.011)	
Civic skills	0.091	(0.007)	†	0.082	(0.014)	†
Recruitment						
Recruitment	0.123	(0.020)	†	0.523	(0.032)	†
Demographics						
Both parents born in United States	0.040	(0.047)				
U.S. citizen				0.847	(0.218)	†
English spoken at home				0.076	(0.105)	
Job status	0.000	(0.052)		0.026	(0.050)	
Retired	0.036	(0.069)		0.554	(0.168)	***
Catholic	−0.037	(0.040)		0.023	(0.074)	
Age	0.003	(0.001)	**			
18–24				−0.382	(0.139)	***
25–34				−0.292	(0.107)	***
35–44				−0.018	(0.101)	
55–64				−0.050	(0.135)	
65 or older				−0.270	(0.170)	
(Constant)	−0.674	(0.140)	†	−2.748	(0.385)	†
Adjusted R-squared	0.42			0.59		
N	1,216			2,083		

SOURCE: Data from the 1996 ANES cross-sectional study and the 1990 American Citizen Participation Study.
[a] In the 1996 ANES model, this variable is measured as detailed in Chapter 3. In the 1990 CPS model, this variable is instrumented. The instruments are education, vocabulary, family income, civic skills, free time, recruitment, U.S. citizenship, English spoken at home, job status, retired, Catholic, 18–24 years old, 25–34 years old, 35–44 years old, 55–64 years old, 65 or older, religious attendance, victim of gender bias, victim of racial bias, victim of religious bias, material dependence on government, problems that government can solve, participation in high school government, job prestige, participation in nonpolitical organizations, and political socialization. See Appendix B and Chapter 4 for more information on variables used in the analysis. The 1996 ANES analysis is weighted by v960003. The 1990 CPS analysis is weighted by wt2517.
$*p < .10$ $**p < .05$ $***p < .01$ $†p < .001$

interest in politics. These results are robust to both datasets and both model specifications. The first analysis, using the 1996 ANES, asks people directly how personally important particular issues are to them. The second analysis, using the 1990 CPS, uses instrumental variables to assess the impact of issue public membership on participation. In both cases, belonging to an issue public has a statistically significant, positive effect on participation.

The strong effect of issue public membership relative to indicators of general interest in politics is quite remarkable, given that conventional measures of political engagement gauge the extent to which an individual has already taken political action in her day-to-day life. Using the 1990 CPS, if we compare people who have the lowest level of political interest with people who have the highest level of interest, the predicted difference in activity levels is slightly more than one political activity. Likewise, someone who is part of an issue public engages in approximately one more activity than someone who is not part of an issue public. The effect of belonging to an issue public is comparable to the effect of political interest. Given that 54 percent of people participate in two or fewer activities and almost 40 percent of people participate in one or fewer activities, a difference of one activity matters. People's personal commitments can push them from being average participators to high participators. This effect is comparable to the difference between someone who never reads the newspaper and has no knowledge of major political figures and someone who is a political news junkie.

Previous studies have argued that "political activity is more a function of beliefs about politics than of specific personal experiences" and that political beliefs "are more a function of general social beliefs than of personal experiences."[16] I find also that political activity can be a function of people's personal issue commitments. Of course people who demonstrate political interest by following the news each day and staying informed about current events are more likely to participate than people who do not. Not everyone, however, connects to politics in this way. Instead of grounding their participation in politicized concerns, some people ground their participation in personal concerns. These personal commitments then animate action. To understand the motivation to participate, we can examine the personal concerns people have instead of examining only generalized levels of political interest, knowledge, and efficacy. Examining generalized political orientations identifies only one set of people who are motivated to participate: those who are already politicized. Examining people's personal concerns identifies a broader group of people who may be involved; those who have a personal commitment may direct their activity toward politics.

HYPOTHESIS 2:
PERSONAL ISSUE COMMITMENTS
HAVE A LARGER EFFECT ON PARTICIPATION
AMONG UNDERRESOURCED INDIVIDUALS

Belonging to an issue public clearly has a direct effect on participation. The second hypothesis asks whether personal issue commitments have a different effect for people with different levels of resources. As shown in Chapter 3, not only the highly educated or very wealthy belong to issue publics. People from various backgrounds can have strong personal commitments to political issues. How do these commitments affect the participation of people from traditionally marginalized backgrounds? What is the relationship between issue public membership and people's personal resources? Is belonging to an issue public more important for people without many participatory resources? Because people like the Montgomery bus boycotters and the Katrina refugees do not have the resources that make participation easier, their barriers to participation are higher. To overcome those barriers, they must have stronger motivations to participate. Thus I expect that personal commitments that drive political action should have a greater impact among people with fewer resources.

To examine the relationship between issue public membership and resources more closely, I run a regression that includes an interaction term between education and issue public membership. This allows me to examine whether the effect of belonging to an issue public varies by education level. I choose education because it arguably gives individuals the ability to decide how much they wish to acquire other financial and civic resources. People who are better educated are more likely to have the option of entering into more lucrative careers. Similarly, people can learn many civic skills through education. Previous research has also shown that education embeds people in social networks that make it easier for them to acquire participatory resources.[17] Income is another possible measure of resources but is perhaps less relevant for many participatory activities. People can be highly educated and choose less financially rewarding careers. Although income matters quite a bit for activities like donating money, it is arguably less important for activities like participating in the community or voting. For those types of activities, things like embeddedness in social networks and knowledge of the political system are key. The regression model is identical to analyses in Table 4.1 except that it includes the interaction term.

Table 4.2 shows the results for both datasets. As with the previous analysis, instrumental variables are used for issue public membership in the CPS to account for the possibility of endogeneity. Consistent with previous analyses, the results show that issue public membership predicts overall participation in activities. The findings with respect to resources, recruitment, and general political motivations are also consistent with previous research. The statistically significant, negative coefficient on the interaction of education and issue public membership shows that the effect of personal issue commitments is particularly strong for people with fewer educational resources.

Figure 4.2 graphs the relationship between personal issue commitments and education using the CPS data. Having strong issue commitments hardly increases the likelihood of participation among people at a higher education level. Participation among those with at least a college degree increases only by about half of one activity (the line is almost flat if we examine people with a postgraduate degree, but only 15 percent of the sample attain that level of education). Among people with less education (those who have not gone further than high school), having an issue commitment can be the difference between participation in one and a half activities and participation in almost four activities. Predicted participation levels rapidly increase, in other words, among those who do not have much education (the effect is even starker for respondents who have only a grammar school education, nearly quadrupling their participation rates, but only 6 percent of the sample falls into that category). Among respondents

TABLE 4.2. Regression of overall activity on personal issue commitments, the interaction of education and personal issue commitments, and other predictors of participation

	1996 American National Elections Study			1990 American Citizen Participation Study		
	B	Std. error		B	Std. error	
Motivation						
Issue commitments[a]	0.33	(0.10)	†	5.73	(2.09)	***
Education * issue commitments[a]	−0.05	(0.02)	***	−1.09	(0.52)	**
Party strength	0.04	(0.02)	*	0.17	(0.04)	†
Political interest	0.19	(0.03)	†	0.20	(0.03)	†
Political knowledge	0.04	(0.02)	*	0.06	(0.02)	**
Political efficacy	0.00	(0.02)		0.06	(0.02)	†
Resources						
Education	0.08	(0.02)	†	0.66	(0.28)	**
Vocabulary				−0.04	(0.02)	*
Household income	0.05	(0.01)	†	0.00	(0.03)	
Free time				0.01	(0.01)	
Civic skills	0.09	(0.01)	†	0.09	(0.02)	†
Recruitment						
Recruitment	0.12	(0.02)	†	0.53	(0.03)	†
Demographics						
Both parents born in United States	0.04	(0.05)				
U.S. citizen				0.84	(0.23)	†
English spoken at home				0.08	(0.11)	
Job status	0.00	(0.05)		0.02	(0.05)	
Retired	0.04	(0.07)		0.53	(0.18)	***
Catholic	−0.04	(0.04)		0.09	(0.09)	
Age	0.00	(0.00)	*			
18–24				−0.47	(0.16)	***
25–34				−0.37	(0.12)	***
35–44				−0.03	(0.11)	
55–64				−0.08	(0.15)	
65 or older				−0.24	(0.18)	
(Constant)	−0.83	(0.15)	†	−4.74	(1.05)	†
Adjusted R-squared	0.43			0.53		
N	1,217			2,083		

SOURCE: Data from the 1996 ANES cross-sectional study and the 1990 American Citizen Participation Study.
[a] In the 1996 ANES model, this variable is measured as detailed in Chapter 3. In the 1990 CPS model, this variable is instrumented. The instruments are education, vocabulary, family income, civic skills, free time, recruitment, U.S. citizenship, English spoken at home, job status, retired, Catholic, 18–24 years old, 25–34 years old, 35–44 years old, 55–64 years old, 65 or older, religious attendance, victim of gender bias, victim of racial bias, victim of religious bias, material dependence on government, problems that government can solve, participation in high school government, job prestige, participation in nonpolitical organizations, and political socialization. See Appendix B and Chapter 4 for more information on variables used in the analysis. The 1996 ANES analysis is weighted by v960003. The 1990 CPS analysis is weighted by wt2517.
$*p < .10$ $**p < .05$ $***p < .01$ $†p < .001$

at the mean education level (those who have at least some college education but no bachelor's degree), the predicted difference between those with and without issue commitments is approximately one and a half activities.

What distinguishes respondents with less education from respondents with high levels of education is the importance of personal issue commitments in explaining differences in who participates. The minimal effects of personal commitments on respondents with more education may emerge for several reasons. Perhaps participation in this population is overdetermined (particularly given the relationship between resources and general motivation that was previously discussed), such that the effect of personal commitments is minimal relative to other factors like resources and general political interest. Perhaps the level of motivation may not vary as much among respondents with higher levels of education. Alternately, differences in motivation may not be as important in explaining variation in participation among that population. No matter what, it appears that

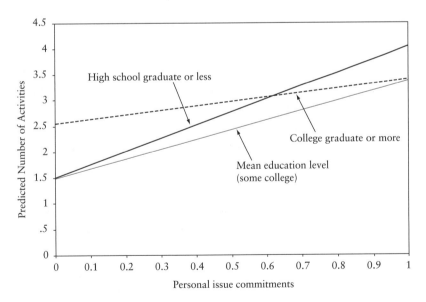

FIGURE 4.2 Predicted participation rates for respondents at different levels of education as the number of issue commitments changes. Lines represent the predicted number of activities a respondent will perform, holding all other variables at their mean. SOURCE: Based on regression analysis of the 1990 American Citizen Participation Study data in Table 4.2.

resources and recruitment are important factors in explaining variation in participation among respondents at all education levels. Among people with low levels of education, however, personal issue commitments are an important factor in explaining differences in participation. People who belong to issue publics are more likely to be motivated to participate, despite having fewer resources.

This analysis points to the importance of understanding motivation to solving problems of political inequality. Because motivation is important for predicting participation among citizens with fewer resources, it becomes important to the effort to remedy persistent inequalities in American politics. People without many participatory resources are in greater need of motivational resources to help them overcome their lack of financial, educational, and civic resources. Bringing more people into the political process, then, entails paying more attention to the personal commitments that can facilitate political action.

UNDERSTANDING THE
MOTIVATION TO PARTICIPATE

Insofar as politics is about the interaction of human beings to achieve a set of collective goals, motivation is at the heart of all of our theories about politics. Whether we are theorizing about the choices voters make in an election, the reasons legislators behave the way they do, or the ways political institutions develop over time, we make assumptions about what individuals want and/or what they are hoping to achieve. These micro-level assumptions guide the logic that leads to other micro- or even more macro-level theories of individual and institutional behavior. Motivation is fundamental to our understanding of political phenomena. Yet, ironically, it is one of the most undertheorized aspects of political behavior.

Even a relatively simple conceptualization of political motivation can help us understand a range of political outcomes. Congressional scholars, for instance, generally assume that elected officials are "single-minded seekers of re-election."[18] Although this one-dimensional view of vote-maximizing politicians ignores the complexity that undoubtedly exists in any elected official's decision-making calculus, it has proven to be analytically useful. With this simple assumption, congressional scholars have explained a variety of institutional and policy outcomes, including multiple aspects of roll-call voting behavior, the development of institutional rules over time, and certain policy outcomes.[19]

A correspondingly simple view of human motivation is not always so fruitful, however. Judicial scholars have long debated the sources of judicial motivation,[20] since simplified assumptions about judges' motives cannot account for a range of observable behaviors. In research on mass politics, a number of studies have found (not surprisingly) that citizens defy easy categorization. The basic assumption about self-interest that guides congressional scholarship does not translate well to citizens, who are generally not as strategic in their behavior.[21] For instance, previous research has shown that voters often support candidates who will not necessarily maximize their economic well-being. Without a more nuanced understanding of motivation, scholars lack an explanation for why people engage in the most fundamental act of democratic citizenship—voting.[22] The varying utility of simplified notions of political motivation in explaining different domains of political behavior has reduced much of the discussion about motivation in political science to a discussion about specific political motivations. Are politicians and voters self-interested actors?

What have been missing from the discussion are the dynamic processes that structure political motivation. Conceptualizing motivation as a process that engages people's personal commitments highlights the importance of personal goals. This chapter showed empirically that alternate ways of thinking about political motivation—in particular, issues that engage people's personal goals—help us better understand who participates. Personal issue commitments can move people to political action. Moving people to take any action is notoriously difficult, and moving people to political action is even harder. Traditional studies of political motivation have argued that people who are politicized in their interests and beliefs will be more likely to act. This chapter argues that although this may be true, they are not the only people who act. People who have strong personal commitments to policy issues can also participate, regardless of the educational, financial, and civic resources they may have.

CHAPTER 5

Pathways to Participation

"CONVERSION STORIES" often appear prominently in discussions of people's religious experiences. In these stories, people who previously were not religious (or perhaps lackadaisical in their commitment) become fervently religious. In his study of political activists, Nathan Teske describes similar experiences for political activists.[1] People who previously were not motivated to pay attention to politics or political issues suddenly shift their orientations. Terence, a college student at the University of Montana in Missoula, describes an incident he covered as a reporter for the college newspaper.[2] Protesting against two hundred Minuteman nuclear missiles stored at a local air force base, a minister conducted an Easter morning service outside the gates of the base. Upon finishing the service, he walked across military security lines and was immediately arrested. Terence says,

> It was like a revelation to me. I saw that this had been happening for centuries [and] that whenever somebody tried to be a peacemaker, and tried to defy the system of war and death, that this is what happened. . . . Then, I looked at where I was—I was on the safe side of the line, writing an article about [the minister]. But all of a sudden I realized that this was a story about me too . . . those nuclear weapons were made by my government too, not just [the minister's]. And I [saw that] I was guilty of the crime of neutrality. I just saw that there were only two sides of the line you could be on. You could be with [the minister] arrested for protesting nuclear weapons, or you could be on the side I was, where everybody . . . gave their unspoken consent to the nuclear arms race. I put down my writing pad and I crossed that line and was arrested.[3]

Like religious converts whose lives are forever changed, Terence's commitment to politics irrevocably changed after this incident. Previously committed to a career in journalism, Terence became a passionate peace activist instead. Once he developed a personal commitment to politics, that commitment motivated him to take action.

What prompts this kind of change? For religious converts and political activists alike, the sources of change are often episodic. Many activists turn to politics as the result of a specific trigger—such as a divorce, a person they met, or a particular event.[4] Some people were raised in highly political families, in which politics was an integral part of life. Some had a teacher in high school who inspired them, while others read books, saw movies, or met people who convinced them that politics was worth their time. Others lived near a landfill or a struggling school system, developing an interest in politics because of their interest in their local communities. Any number of specific life experiences can generate political commitment. Do we have to rely on unpredictable life circumstances and events to motivate participation, however? Or are there more systematic patterns to how people are motivated?

This chapter examines the pathways that lead people to participation. Although some previous research has examined whether or not people are motivated or what people's motivations are, there has been very little research examining *how* people become motivated to participate in politics. In part, this lack of research stems from the belief that people's motivations emerge for episodic, idiosyncratic reasons. Interviews with fifty-eight politically active individuals reveal distinct commonalities in the ways that people get involved. Commonalities in participation pathways emerge even though the people are from different parts of the country, are from different backgrounds, and have been involved with politics in a range of different ways. This chapter examines these pathways, tracing the common themes that emerge.

Recognizing the commonalities in people's pathways opens the possibility of finding systematic ways to generate personal commitments that motivate participation. Insofar as these personal commitments make participation more likely among traditionally marginalized populations, increasing people's motivation can help reduce inequality in American politics. If more underresourced people can be motivated to participate, then a broader range of people may be represented and inequalities may decline. However, relying on biographical events—such as meeting a role model, moving to a new community, or experiencing a sudden life change—to generate political motivation is too random to contribute to systematic reform. Increasing the number of people who have strong personal commitments to politics depends on finding ways to generate motivation systematically.

UNDERSTANDING PATHWAYS TO PARTICIPATION

What determines who is in an issue public and who is not? Why does one person care passionately about abortion policy, while another person does not care about politics at all? Why does one person focus on environmental policy, while another person focuses on U.S. policy toward the Middle East? The sources of issue public membership, and political motivation more broadly, are relatively diverse. People can develop strong personal commitments to politics in a number of different ways. Previous research has focused primarily on the kinds of experiences that can politicize people's orientations, but not on the processes by which that politicization occurs.

Previous research on the origins of issue public membership argues that it originates from three main sources: concerns about an individual's material well-being, her social network, or her values.[5] Some people's concern for policy originates out of self-interest. An example of this is farmers who are concerned about farm policy. Because government policies have a clear and direct impact on farmers' economic well-being, they are often quite aware of and active on farm policy issues.[6] Other people care about an issue because they identify socially with a group of people who are active on that issue. The concern of pro-life advocates regarding abortion may have originated from their interaction with peers and leaders from their church. Finally, people may care about issues that are consistent with their values or with their vision of the kind of people they want to be.[7] For example, a person might be passionate about environmental policy because she values her role as a steward of natural resources.

Vincent Hutchings examines the role that political context can play in activating issue publics in *Public Opinion and Democratic Accountability*.[8] He argues that political elites can shape the activity of issue publics by providing information about what representatives are doing—or not doing. Although he does not focus on the question of motivation, he argues that people become activated when they realize that their elected representatives are not behaving in ways that they desire. According to Hutchings's model, people become selectively activated around issues in part because elite political actors and institutions selectively provide information about what legislators are doing. When legislators take actions contrary to public wishes, "the mass media, interest group leaders, and potential challengers become alerted, thereby increasing the likelihood that interested voters will become informed."[9] People's motivation to get involved depends on what the media, interest group leaders, and electoral challengers choose to emphasize. Political context thus can shape issue public membership through information flows, which determine what issues are on the political agenda and what information people have about the ways that politics intersects with their personal lives.

Studies of political socialization have broadened this research to look not only at the sources of issue public membership but also at the sources of lifelong political orientations. In a research review, Virginia Sapiro defines political socialization as "research on the patterns and processes by which individuals engage in political development and learning, constructing their particular relationships to the political contexts in which they live."[10] Socialization research has found that patterns of political discussion and activity at home, and civic and political experiences as youth, can shape lifelong orientations toward politics.[11] Likewise, children who have teachers who incorporate teaching about politics often develop lifelong political identities and skills.[12] In his study of activists in the civil rights movement, Doug McAdam finds that people's reasons for becoming involved often depended on a set of life circumstances, including the presence of material resources, role models, a support network, and accessible avenues for participation.[13]

Scholars find that these early experiences can explain continuities in political orientations over time, despite changing life circumstances and distinctly different behaviors.[14] Helen Haste and Judith Torney-Purta call this "political awareness" and argue that each individual has a certain framework that she brings to interpreting the world.[15] This framework determines how she infuses meaning into and interprets the political world and, hence, her individual orientation toward political participation. Teske calls this an "Identity Construction Model," in which people are motivated to participate because it is consistent with their perceptions of themselves: "Identity construction points to the qualitative concerns and desires activists have that certain qualities be instantiated in their actions and lives."[16] Teske argues that the process of participation itself helps activists construct identities for themselves, which they then are motivated to sustain through their future actions. This is similar to Joanne Miller and Wendy Rahn's approach, which argues that people have "public identities" that affect political behavior through the "logic of appropriateness" and "emotional arousal."[17] Instead of making a strategic calculation about whether or not participation will help an individual reach her goals, she participates because it seems "appropriate," given her sense of self. Alternately, commitment to a particular public identity can lead to emotional arousal when certain events, individuals, or other political phenomena touch emotional chords. In both theories, people participate because it is consistent with their identity.

A key point emerging from this literature is that people's orientations and commitments toward politics are constructed from their life experiences. Whether people base their commitments in their material well-being, their social networks, or other biographical experiences, their commitments emerge from their interactions with the world. People are not born with predetermined levels of political motivation. Individual life experiences inevitably shape a person's motivation.[18] People develop interests, identities, and motivations over time as they experience politics through their relationships with the people and the world around them. In part, this occurs because social interactions crucially affect people's interpretations of the world. Often, people's perceptions of a situation are strongly influenced by the people around them.[19]

Familiar and trusted people (like parents and teachers) can play a crucial role in determining a young person's interpretations of and reactions to politics. Imagine a child's first exposure to politics. Is the canvasser knocking at the door someone to welcome or someone to turn away? Lacking prior information about how to react, the child will look to cues from her parents or try to infer from similar situations how she should react.[20] If her parents warmly welcome the individual, the child will record a different impression of politics from the one recorded if her parents slam the door and make snide comments about political canvassers. This information begins to form the basis of her subsequent reactions to politics.[21] Over time, the child will or will not develop an interest in politics. Each individual has a unique constellation of experiences that form the basis of political motivation. Some people may be raised in environments that make them very likely to be engaged in politics while others are raised in environments that do not. Early experiences play a crucial role in determining how committed a person may be to politics.

Most research on the sources of issue public membership or political socialization does not consider the development of political orientations in terms of the choices an individual can make. Researchers examine experiences that have the potential to create lifelong political orientations, but they do not examine the choices people actually make to take that path. Participating in politics, however, is a choice. For example, research has shown that people who grow up in highly political families are much more likely to become political themselves. Yet not everyone who grows up in that kind of family grows up to be political. Similarly, we know that people who have had meaningful civic experiences in high school are more likely to have lifelong political orientations than people who did not—but not everyone who had those experiences has a political orientation later in life. Why do some people choose political action and others do not? In their study of union leaders, Marshall Ganz et al. assert that social action is shaped by "intentionality and purpose."[22] In their studies of activists, both McAdam and Teske point out that political activists often perceive themselves as having taken an unusual life path and that they are quick to defend their motivations for doing so.[23] People who participate in politics, whether it involves attending a neighborhood meeting or devoting a life to political activism, all make the choice to participate. Previous research tells us what factors make it more likely that people will make that choice, but we do not yet know the pathways that people take toward those choices.

THE STUDY OF POLITICAL PATHWAYS

To develop a better understanding of the pathways people take to participation, I interviewed fifty-eight individuals in the spring and summer of 2008 about their participation in politics. The Study of Political Pathways was designed to uncover the processes by which people became involved in politics, the paths they took, and the choices they made along the way. The study is purely descriptive and is not intended to make any causal claims about what leads people to participation. It seeks to identify common themes and ideas by examining the choices that fifty-eight disparate individuals made about how and when to participate in public life. Interestingly, although these individuals came from varied backgrounds, participated in varied ways, and were from different generations and regions of the country, there were common themes in the paths they took.

Despite limitations for generalizability and replication, in-depth interviews can provide insights that simple survey data do not. Given the range of ways people can become involved in politics—from socialization processes, to role models and mentors, to personal experiences of injustice and other experiences too numerous to list—surveys with closed-ended questions have difficulty tracing the paths that people take to political involvement. For example, surveys can ask whether people have had particular types of experiences, but are less effective in adjudicating between those experiences to determine which ones were most important in triggering action. Open-ended interviews allow the questions and conversation to be tailored to the experiences the subjects describe, and they provide room for follow-up questions and additional probing when necessary. Many subjects traced a clear path in which one experience led to another, and the choice to get involved in politics was clearest with an understanding of the sequential order of events. Thus we can develop a richer picture of the ways people get involved. In addition, when asked about something as broad as their reasons for getting involved, most subjects began with broad generalizations but became more specific as they were given time to "think out loud." These ideas emerged only through the format of open-ended discussions. The downsides of this kind of data are that replication is difficult and it is unclear how generalizable the results are. Replication is an important standard for scientific research, but so is addressing important substantive questions. These standards sometimes come into conflict with each other, as certain methods allow us only to address certain questions. Generalizability is impossible without probability sampling, but we can still compare our sample to other samples of political participants on commonly used dimensions (such as education and income).

The sample was constructed as a "snowball sample."[24] I began by selecting different types of membership-based civic and political organizations that worked in a variety of issue areas in different parts of the country on both sides of the political spectrum. I strove to achieve organizational diversity in the kinds of issues the organizations focused on, the types of work they did, and the regions of the country in which they operated. I oversampled among organizations working with immigrant and underprivileged communities, since I was particularly interested in the processes by which people without many resources got involved in politics. After compiling a list of organizations, I asked them for their help in recruiting members for participation in the study. Some organizations allowed me to post a notice in a newsletter or on their membership Listserv. Other organizations helped me identify and recruit individual members willing to participate in the interview. I also leveraged my personal network to locate potential interviewees and asked subjects at the end of the interview if they knew of any other people I should interview. After identifying names of people, I would call or e-mail them to invite them to participate in the study. Through this method, I identified and interviewed fifty-eight people.

Although this sample is in no way representative of people who participate in politics or even of political activists, it did incorporate a diverse range of people. The study includes people who were active in a variety of areas, such as (in no particular order) immigration organizations, environmental organizations, neighborhood organizations, human rights organizations, political campaigns, education organizations, community service organizations, pro-life organizations, pro-choice organizations, labor unions, religious organizations, minority rights organizations, local government, international development, women's groups, and a range of community-based groups. Involvement in politics ranged widely among the subjects, from those who held full-time paid positions in political advocacy organizations to those who participated only intermittently by donating money or voting. Because of how the sample was constructed, it was skewed toward people who were affiliated with a particular civic or political organization or campaign. The sample included more people who were politically liberal than were politically conservative, simply because liberal organizations turned out to be more receptive to my requests for help.

Table 5.1 compares the demographic characteristics of people interviewed in the Study of Political Pathways with those of respondents in the 1990 American Citizen Participation Study. The 1990 CPS specifically looks at people who are involved in public life in some way and therefore provides a useful comparison point for the pathways study. The key difference between the two is that the Study of Political Pathways over-samples immigrants (those who were born outside the United States or have at least one parent born outside the United States), minorities, and women. I deliberately oversampled among these groups because I was interested in observing the ways people from communities with less voice in the political process get involved. Respondents from both studies are comparable in terms of average household income (once adjusted for inflation), the percentage working full-time, and age. The two studies have about a 10-percentage-point difference in the share of respondents with

TABLE 5.1. Comparison of demographic characteristics of respondents in the 2008 Study of Political Pathways and the 1990 American Citizen Participation Study

	2008 Study of Political Pathways	1990 American Citizen Participation Study
% born in United States	71.2%	93.4%
% with both parents born in United States	54.2%	83.9%
% minority	38.9%	16.7%
% female	64.8%	52.7%
% working full-time	53.7%	56.2%
Average household income*	$50,000–59,999	$30,000–34,999
% with college degree	40.7%	31.0%
Average age	41.8	43.5

SOURCE: Data from the 2008 Study of Political Pathways and the 1990 American Citizen Participation Study.
*Income numbers are not adjusted for inflation.

a college degree. Between 1990 and 2007, however, U.S. Census data show that there was approximately an 8-percentage-point increase in the proportion of people completing four years of college.[25] The difference between the two samples in educational attainment parallels changes in the broader society.

The interviews were all in-depth, semistructured interviews conducted by me or a research assistant. Although we did have a set of questions that served as an interview protocol (see Appendix C for the specific questions), the interviews were free-flowing conversations. All of the interviews began with a consent form, to ensure that interviewees understood the goal of the study and that their participation was voluntary, and ended with a set of demographic questions. Beyond that, the structure was flexible. All the interviews covered the questions included on the protocol, but the questions were asked in different orders and in different ways depending on how the conversation flowed. For the most part, interviewees were quite forthcoming about their past and current involvement and allowed us to ask some very personal questions. The interviews were generally about forty-five minutes long but ranged from as short as twenty minutes to as long as an hour and forty minutes.

Because the interviews are all self-reports, the question arises whether people are able to report on their own pathways to participation. Certainly there has been much debate about whether people can accurately report their own motivations. Are the retrospective accounts they give of their own actions credible? Schlozman, Verba, and Brady claim that they are, particularly since they vary "sensibly" across modes of activity.[26] Others argue that people's retrospective accounts of their own motivations are nothing more than rationalizations for actions they have taken and that such accounts may or may not reflect what was motivating them at the time.[27] This study thus moves away from asking people what their motivations were and instead asks about the process by which they became involved. We began by asking people to describe their involvement, and then we probed to find out exactly how they got to that place. We asked people to tell us specific things, such as how they found the organization, how they figured out where the meeting was, whether someone recruited them, what they did at these meetings, and so on. We found that although many interviewees began with rather broad descriptions of why they were involved (for example, they believed in giving back to their communities), they became more specific once we began asking them about the process. Whether or not people are reliable reporters of their own motivations, they do seem to be able to report the specific steps they took to get involved.

One drawback of this sample is that it does not include anyone who is *not* involved in civic or political life. Preliminary pilot testing indicated that most people do not make an active choice to be uninvolved in public life. Instead, they neglect voting, going to the neighborhood meeting, or otherwise being involved because they are too busy, they forget, or life otherwise gets in the way. Because it is not an active choice to be uninvolved, it is harder to discern a pathway (or the lack thereof). People who are involved, in contrast, all had to make an explicit choice at some point to become involved and are thus better able to reflect on and discuss that choice. The difficulty people have in discussing their lack of involvement in politics underscores two key points: First, the choice people make to get involved is important. Second, many people who believe that involvement in public life is important (i.e., those who hold those expressive values) do not actually get involved. Having those values is not enough.

THREE KEY THEMES

The central finding of the Study of Political Pathways is that the development of people's issue commitments is not completely idiosyncratic. Clear themes and patterns emerged in the accounts of subjects' pathways to participation. Whether people first got involved and subsequently chose to stay involved depended critically on the actions of other people, organizations, or campaigns. Three themes emerged. First, values in the absence of a triggering experience that personalized politics are not enough to motivate action. People from all backgrounds reported having altruistic, instrumental, and expressive values, but having those values was not enough to prompt participation. Subjects often reported that a specific event or experience triggered their choice to take action. Second, people's commitment to issues often grew out of their participation, which has implications for causality that will be explored below. They often reported getting involved initially for alternate reasons. Third, people said their choice to get involved and stay involved often depended on what their early experiences with participation were like. What the organizations or campaigns did mattered.

Theme 1: Without a Triggering Experience That Personalizes Politics, Values Alone Are Not Enough To Motivate Action

Believing in something and doing something about it are not the same. Consistent with previous research, subjects expressed a wide range of goals that motivated them to get involved, including instrumental, relational, and expressive goals. The element of their stories that has been ignored in previous research is that they all had a particular experience that triggered their political action. Many people have broad values but do not act on them. People often need a triggering experience to see how political action can help them fulfill personal goals and values.

Most subjects reported that a combination of factors led to their participation: an abstract goal or value that they were trying to fulfill and a specific experience or goal that triggered actual action. In many cases, the abstract goal was expressive, centering on people's altruistic motivations or feelings of civic duty. The concrete, personal experience often led to specific goals that were instrumental—a desire to achieve a concrete end (such as affecting policy on a particular issue) through their participation. As Teske found in his research, subjects did not see the juxtaposition of these two types of goals as incongruous.[28] In fact, both seemed necessary to motivate action. The abstract value acted as a priming agent, preparing subjects for the possibility of getting involved and showing them models of how they might do so. The specific event was necessary to move people to choose action. Both the abstract values and the triggering events were constructed from people's personal experiences. Subjects all pointed to specific life experiences that resulted in their having certain values and to other experiences that pushed them into taking action.

In discussing abstract values that drove them to get involved, many subjects expressed a general sense that contributing to society was important. The expression of these values varied by people's backgrounds. Subjects who came from more privileged backgrounds expressed a belief in the importance of giving something back. As Carrie, the daughter of a doctor and a lawyer, put it,

I was definitely raised with the concept that it was a requirement. If you have so much given to you, if you have an education, for all that you have been given, you have a duty to repay society. . . . I was raised with the idea [from] my parents—well, really my father—that you work for what you have and then you give back. [That is] how a successful society functions. . . . When [my father] was a child, he was a foster child. He was taken in by people who didn't have to, but thought it would be good for society to raise children who are without any parents. It is not like we had foster children when we were growing up, but [we had] that same concept of giving back.

Subjects from less privileged backgrounds often expressed their values in terms of social justice. They felt they had a responsibility to fight against an injustice that they may have perceived in their own lives and may have seen others experience. Jose grew up in a family that was, as he put it, "dirt poor in a very privileged community." Witnessing this contrast helped him develop the sense that he wanted to fight against it:

We lived in an apartment complex with the rest of the [poor] kids . . . while almost everybody else had houses. In high school everybody had a car—I didn't. I can name example after example . . . that is there right from the beginning—I was told to assimilate or else, because you're different. . . . So then finding my own identity and having that inner fight for it . . . I'm supposed to be different, but everybody here is different so why can't I have my own life? This whole personal piece is that I think everybody should be able to lead their life the way they want. . . . So I think there is [a] strong piece of that—that once I started to see inequality, I wanted to do something about it because of my own personal experience.

Other subjects expressed their values in terms of an appreciation for society's potential to help people. Immigrants and people who had some international experience—whether it be having lived abroad or having intimate knowledge of another society—were most likely to express their values in these terms. Rahul, the son of two immigrants, said,

I really believe in America. I believe in the idea of it. . . . I feel as though there really is a mission we have as a country. . . . Yeah, my parents came here when they were thirty or twenty-eight or so. My snap reaction is that America is the greatest country in the world; my father always said that. My mom was always more ambivalent, but through her actions she said the same thing. Like my dad, though, would say that this is the greatest country in the world and this will always be the greatest country in the world. He mostly said it in reference to people becoming rich. He said it in terms of rags to riches—look at Bill Clinton's story. [My dad's] a huge Republican, but he recognizes that you can really make something of yourself here, like Bill Gates. "Look at me. I don't make a ton of money, but I live comfortably. Look at your mom . . ." He would say this in bits and pieces. He felt really strongly that we were a country that could make people's dreams come true. I think that inspired me.

Most subjects stated that contributing to the public good was somehow important to them. Whether they expressed it as giving back, fighting injustice, or living up to the potential of the American dream, this expressive value was part of what motivated their participation.

The finding that people's expression of values varied by their background is consistent with the idea that goals and values are shaped by life experiences. They are neither innate nor spontaneously emergent. Instead, they develop through experience. Subjects described varied sources of their values that are largely consistent with the findings in the literature on political socialization.[29] Family members (including parents, grandparents, and other close family members) were an important source of values. Many subjects described growing up in families or communities where civic and political participation was modeled for them. Virginia, an older woman who is actively involved in local politics in her community, describes the origins of her commitment to public work:

I grew up during the Depression, and I have two memories. We lived next to my grandparents and we were less affected by it. I remember being on my bike and seeing the young men who would come around begging for something to eat, and my grandmother would give them a sandwich. I think it had enough calories for the whole day. The message was, we feed the hungry. [I also] remember going on a field trip in third grade, field trips then must have cost all of fifty cents, which is actually proportionally more than it is now, and my father gave me an extra fifty cents for the boy who lived in our backyard. He told me to give the fifty cents to the teacher when no one was around and tell her it was for [the boy] and not to tell him it came from me, but he was to go on the field trip. Was he trying to teach me a lesson, or did he just want to make sure [the boy] got to go? I don't know. But we definitely do reach out and try to help other people.

Family was not the only source of values. Some described nonfamilial role models, including teachers, mentors, and inspiring public figures. Some cited religion, books, and other educational experiences. Naomi witnessed people helping her in her own life. Raised by a single mother who was an immigrant, Naomi relied on many other people as she was growing up.

I think for me the reason I knew I wanted to help people was because of all these people who have helped me along the way because I came from a single-parent family. So I knew a lot more personally that it takes a lot more than one person helping you. So for me it's about everyone—every path or road that I took, people were lending me a hand to get me ahead.

Many people developed an abstract sense of wanting to help the community, give back to others, or be civically involved by watching family members, teachers, or other role models or learning about this value through books, school, and other experiences.

Simply having abstract goals (such as the ideal of civic duty), however, was not enough to motivate actual action. Subjects in these interviews reported needing more than just a set of abstract goals to get them motivated. Jane expressed her commitment to altruistic values:

I think it's important to give back to the community. . . . [It's] important as a value that you give what you receive. Right now, even though you always have your hands full with other things, I just think it's important to give to your community, to your family, to your friends, and the circle just goes out and out.

But when asked how she participates, she says, "[I] just listen to the radio. That's the extent of it, just being as involved as I might like to be." Later, she admits to wanting to be more involved, but she does not have the impetus to actually do it.

I'm not as informed as I would like to be. I wish I read more newspapers and magazines and had more things in the house consistently. It's one of those things I know I should do but don't always do.

Mere exposure to abstract values is not enough. Subjects who all expressed a commitment to giving back to the community in the examples above had varying levels of involvement in politics. Carrie volunteers with a community service organization two hours a week and is not very involved with politics. Jose has chosen a career in which he works full-time for a community service and political advocacy organization. Rahul maintains an active interest in politics and occasionally donates money to campaigns but is not involved in civic or political life in any consistent way. Simply believing that giving back to the community is important or that participation is part of one's civic duty does not necessarily predict high levels of participation. As one of the interviewees noted, there are many instances in which siblings are exposed to the same values in their families but do not take the same paths toward participation. Aissa reports being involved in politics because she has always believed it is important to speak out against injustice. According to her, her father was the source of these values. Yet she asks,

Why me? I have six siblings who are not that far [from me in age] and then three siblings who are a lot younger. Within the six siblings I can say, why me? Why did I choose to go down that path [toward activism]?

Although she and her siblings were all exposed to the same set of values from her father, none of her siblings internalized them in the same way to become politically active like Aissa. Many of the subjects had similar stories of friends, peers, or siblings who were exposed to the same values but did not make the same choices. What made the difference for these subjects?

Most subjects made the choice to participate when an event, experience, or person connected political action directly to their personal goals. Kevin, for example, grew up in a politically active family, and his father ran for elected office twice while he was a child. Although he says that "politics was something that I was very much interested in since I had been a kid," Kevin had hardly been involved as an adult until he made a more personal connection. He first got involved in electoral politics when a candidate with AIDS ran for elected office. In describing his motives for getting involved, Kevin says, "Well, I just think it was the personal connection or what seemed to be a personal connection because our nephew had died of AIDS." Despite a long-standing family commitment to politics, Kevin still needed the personal connection to take action. Another subject, Mary, describes her motivations for being involved in terms of the needs she has in her personal life.

I was a single parent, I was putting myself through school as a single parent on welfare and financial aid, loans and whatever. . . . But it was me trying to meet my needs for me and my child. Because I needed community, I needed family, I needed support services, I needed a way to provide her with a culturally appropriate way for her to exist in the world. . . . For me it's about dealing with the stuff that affects me.

She got involved to correct problems of perceived injustice in her own life. This woman had been raised in a community of people who had been civically active, but she herself never chose to get involved until there was an issue that directly affected her and her daughter's lives. Another subject, Antonio, works as a political organizer for an immigration advocacy organization and describes his reasons for being involved as centrally tied to the implications his work has for his own life.

I started becoming more of a leader in the organization about six months after I first got involved. I realized going to a weekly meeting and going to rallies wasn't enough for me. I wanted more. I realized this was not only going to affect my life, but my sister's life and the students that I am around. That is when I went back to the office and was like, "What do you want me to do? I will do anything. I want to volunteer." I kept coming back, coming back, and I kept being given more leadership and more responsibilities.

Antonio had to make the personal connection between politics and his own life before he became truly committed to immigration work. Such triggering events are tied to personal goals.

Many people expressed their values in terms of the impact they saw political involvement having in their own life and the lives of the people around them. For instance, one subject described growing up in the 1960s and seeing the Black Panther Party actively working in his neighborhood: "These men were dating my sisters . . . and some of them were involved with the Black Panther Party, some of them were involved with street organizations that at the time were trying to make a difference in the lives of my sisters and brothers." Many subjects became involved because they witnessed the consequences of inaction in their own neighborhoods. They got involved with a clear hope of changing the situation. Alma says,

Because this is where I live, this is where my family lives, this is where my daughter lives, this is where we have all grown up and we are all going to keep growing, like my little cousins and everything. It is important to change it now, especially with the chain of violence that is going on. It is like every week that you hear somebody new got shot and you are going to someone else's funeral, and you know everyone 'cause they are just older than you, like twenty, twenty-one, eighteen. We know we have to do something because no one else is stepping up.

Alma was motivated to get involved because she cared about her community. People made the choice to participate once abstract values took more concrete form in their lives, and they became motivated to actually take action.

A variety of experiences could trigger subjects' choice to take action. Community service work, education, or personal experiences of injustice, for example, galvanized their interest in a particular issue or participation in general. In many cases, the trigger was not political but personal. The trigger was often another person. As much previous research has shown, recruitment works.[30] Many subjects described first getting involved in politics because someone else recruited them or because they wanted to support a close friend or family member. Simply being asked matters. In describing why he joined a men's group that was pivotal in galvanizing his future participation, Justin says, "I was invited. . . . It was that simple. This guy I knew asked me if I wanted to come to one of the meetings." The invitation was particularly powerful when it came from a role model. Rahul describes the professor who first invited him to attend a meeting of a political organization on campus: "She was so cool; it was so classic, the freshman being wowed by a professor." People's social relationships, whether with peers or role models, often played important roles in triggering their initial participation. Andrew, a twenty-six-year-old political activist, describes first getting involved with political action in high school to support a friend: "Certainly some of the initial organizations I got involved in in high school, like the Gay-Straight Alliance—that was just a direct relationship because it was started by one of my close friends. She had recently come out as a lesbian." Similarly, when asked why she first volunteered at a crisis pregnancy center, Wendy notes that it was to help a friend, even though she did not enjoy the work: "[I got involved because of] quite a few of the gals at our church. In fact, my close friend was the director. . . . She was always mentioning that they had a need for counselors. So I did that, but I never felt as strongly." People got involved to support someone else or because someone recommended that they should. Although they would first go to a meeting, start volunteering, or otherwise get involved because a friend or a teacher suggested it, these early experiences got their foot in the door and often led to further participation.

Other subjects, particularly those from underprivileged backgrounds, perceived personal experiences of injustice in their own lives, which pushed them to get active in an effort to correct the injustice. John, an African-American male, became an election monitor after seeing his wife mistreated at the polls.

My wife lived in a part where there were these very racist elections, racist judges and captains. She went to vote one day and they treated her like crap, and I thought, "I am going to change this." . . . I started going to community meetings on how to change it, and I did. I got involved with the political organizations in the neighborhood.

Caesar had not been very politically active or aware until he realized that he might be blocked from fulfilling one of his personal dreams:

I'm here in the U.S. undocumented. It has been my dream to go to college since I was a sophomore in high school, but because of the fact that I'm undocumented here in the U.S., I'm forced to pay out-of-state tuition, which is usually twice or three times what a regular student would pay. So I became involved in politics that way. I wanted to advocate for getting in-state tuition here in [name of state] because I've been living here basically for eight years now. First my history teacher put me in touch with [name of immigrant advocacy organization], and I started volunteering there.

Both Caesar and John had specific experiences in which they or people close to them felt unfairly excluded from the system. This sense of unfairness prompted them to take action. Andrew, on the other hand, was not from an underprivileged background but nonetheless was motivated by a specific instance of perceived injustice. He talks about how his commitment to participating increased:

Through other organizations, I went to major demonstrations during that time. I personally witnessed and personally experienced some nasty behavior by the police—coming at me with a baton while I was walking away from him. . . . So you kind of say a picture is worth a thousand words—but that experience drove home the point of what an ugly system, for lack of a better word, we are actually living in.

Witnessing injustice in their own lives or in the lives of loved ones prompted Caesar, John, and Andrew to get involved. Alejandra was a bit different because she felt that although she had found the resources she needed in her own life, not everyone around her was so lucky:

I think even though a lot of things have to relate back to me, it's "me" in a different way because I went to high school, and just because I did things the way I did, I knew I was going to be fine . . . but I had a lot of people in my family who did not, and I see the struggle and I see what's going on. I see my brother . . . and he's an example of the failed system, I see my cousins who are involved in things that are not so great, and I know the paths that I could have taken. . . . I know that even though I didn't have all the resources that I needed, I did use those that I had, and not everyone can do that.

Although Alejandra felt as if she had been successful in her own life, she perceived systemic pressures that made it difficult for people around her. Recognizing these pressures in the lives of her brother and her cousins became the source of her motivation. Like Alejandra, many of the subjects in this study did not choose action until they had a specific problem in their lives that they wanted to solve.

In some cases, a triggering event or experience helped subjects imagine the possibility of a different life. Only by seeing the possibility of something different did they become motivated to take action. Jamal, a thirty-seven-year-old African-American man who volunteers with a political campaign, said,

You know, here is the thing: so let's say you are a ten-year-old kid and you grew up in your family and all you see is drugs and alcohol and abusive parents or nonexistent parents or whatever it is—this is all you know. But then you meet a teacher who tells you about her experiences, which I did [names teacher], and about going to Pakistan and Vietnam and how she had done all these trips. So I remember being a kid and saying to myself—I swear to you I remember saying, "Maybe drugs are not the answer. Maybe there is something else." I don't know what the something else was but . . . all I remember thinking was, "If this is the example of what there is, then there must be something else."

For many subjects, this ability to imagine a different set of circumstances came through their involvement. Caesar notes that he stayed involved with an immigrant rights organization because it was the first time he realized there was a way that he could go to college. Betty, who initially got involved in public life by working in the school system to help her children, says that she "learned a lot" from working with "powerful" women who helped her realize that, as a woman, she could be very active. Imagining a set of circumstances different from their own motivated these subjects to stay involved.

Although most subjects identified broad values that motivated them, those values were often not enough to generate actual action. Almost all of the subjects were able, without prompting, to name specific events, people, or experiences through which they made the connection between their values and political action. The importance of that triggering event, as well as the grounding of people's values in their life experiences, underscores the idea that motivation is constructed through interaction with the world.

Theme 2: Issue Commitments Emerge Through Participation

Because most subjects in the study were affiliated with a civic or political organization, most also were personally concerned with particular issues and thus were members of some issue public. These issues ranged from broad policy concerns, like abortion policy, to specific concerns about local issues, such as the construction of a youth center in the neighborhood. As predicted in the previous chapters, these subjects identified these issues as important motivators of their participation. Yet their participation did not always *begin* with a commitment to these issues. In many cases, subjects' commitment to the issues grew out of their participation.

This theme immediately raises questions about causality. How can issue commitments grow out of people's participation if, as shown in the previous chapter, issue commitments predict participation? We can make a distinction between two choices people make in participating in politics. First, people make the decision to get involved for the first time. How or why did the individual decide to attend her first meeting, get informed about a particular issue, or get to know a new person who became her link to participation? Second, how or why did the person decide to stay involved? For most subjects, these were two separate choices. The descriptive analysis of subjects' self-reports shows that while issue commitments may or may not have played a role in the first decision, they often played a role in the second decision. The analysis in the previous chapter was careful to address issues of causality in examining the impact of issue commitments in motivating ongoing participation. Subjects in this study reported issue commitments as being important motivators of participation, but they were not always the reason that people first got involved.

Why did subjects first get involved if they did not have specific issue commitments? In many cases, alternate goals drove their action. These goals played the same role of connecting political action to their personal concerns, but the personal concerns were often not very political. The goals ranged from doing something for their children, to social networking, to wanting to have fun. In each case, these people did not get involved in public life with the goal of participating in the political system—instead, they got involved because they wanted to improve their children's education, they wanted new friends, or they saw a learning opportunity for their own careers.

Fulfilling alternate goals pushes people to first get involved with public life, and that initial involvement often leads to further involvement with an issue. Some people get involved with clear instrumental goals, such as furthering their professional careers. Frank says, "For some people it's about reputation. When you meet people, they help you build your reputation . . . getting involved in the community is a way to do that." Elizabeth, an environmental activist who works for an environmental advocacy organization, initially got involved not because of an interest in the environment, but because she wanted to learn computer skills:

So I would say that there were two motivations that got me involved in the [environmental organization]. The first one was I saw sort of a personal opportunity for me to use skills that I had in a new way. I had never edited a newsletter before, and it was right when . . . Macintoshes were brand-new, and the whole world of desktop publishing—PageMaker, Quark, those were brand-new programs—and [this organization] had them, and I could use the skills I had as a graphic designer with [them]. [They also] had these new programs, PageMaker, that I never used before, and I thought, "Oh cool, I'll learn something myself." This was an advantage to me to learn to use these programs . . . I had met the people, and I thought these are people I like. I thought, "These are people I could hang with, I could work with." So it was a combination of the people and the skills and the actual topic of environmental work that was something like the third on my list. "Oh, that's okay. Oh, I believe in this stuff. . . . No reason not to." . . . I like the environment, even though I had never really done anything before for the environment other than, you know, recycle.

When Elizabeth initially got involved, she had only a fleeting commitment to environmental goals and environmental activism. She was interested in using the graphic design skills she already had and learning new ones. She was also new to the area and wanted to build some social connections. Environmentalism was not something to which she objected, and she would be "happy to help them out," but it was far from her primary objective in getting involved.

A number of women described first getting involved in the community to improve their children's education, including Betty, a fervent sixty-three-year-old political activist:

The first, most significant involvement I had was when my oldest daughter, who is forty-one now, was three, and we were at the Montessori school, and they were so strict about not using anything that wasn't started by Maria Montessori that we broke off and started a different school. . . . [With] three other parents, we started a school that met our needs. . . . We weren't gonna be restricted.

Similarly, Susan ran for elected office to be a member of town meeting because she was upset by the quality of education her children were receiving.

The high school was falling apart, but we knew the schools were amazing. People wanted to renovate the high school, but people didn't want their property taxes to go up. I took a tour of the high school, and I was like [this is happening] in [name of hometown]. So I ended up running for town meeting. . . . It was 1994. For two years I was involved. A bunch of us did a slate together. We were voted on by precinct. . . . I think I selfishly wanted this override [on property taxes] to happen.

Neither Betty nor Susan expressed strong political interest prior to her involvement with her children's education, but after experiencing the value of collective action, or getting involved in town politics, both women eventually got involved in other types of activity as well.

Not all people expressed clearly "purposive" personal goals. Some wanted social solidarity or recreation. A number of subjects described initially getting involved for social reasons. They wanted to be involved in activities with their friends or to find friends who shared their interests and values. As Katie put it, "I needed to find some people who were like minded. . . . I guess it was kind of a support group in a way, so I guess that is what really motivated me to get involved." Rebecca says, "I don't have much altruism in my personality. I like to connect to things and people I like, and I like doing things that I think [are] fun." For many of these people, commitment to the political or ideological goals of the organization they joined was secondary to the desire to fulfill the alternate goal.

The importance of alternate goals is consistent with previous research, which finds that people join civic and political organizations for a wide range of reasons that may or may not be tied to the political goals of the organization.[31] People may have political goals, but they may also want to meet new people, develop their leadership skills, or find new recreational activities. Particularly given that many interest groups offer selective incentives (or alternate material incentives) to persuade people to join,[32] it is clear that members of an interest group are not necessarily passionate about that issue. Individuals may join AARP (American Association of Retired Persons) because they care deeply about government provision of services to seniors or because they simply want to receive the travel discounts AARP provides for members. Conversely, a citizen may care deeply about environmental issues but may not join the Sierra Club because she does not like the local group in her area. People who belong to interest groups are not necessarily people who care personally about political issues, and people who care personally about political issues may not belong to interest groups. Being committed to an issue does not have to be tied to being part of an organized interest group.

A 2003 study of Sierra Club activists provides some evidence that people become active in political organizations for a wide range of reasons.[33] The Sierra Club is a leading national environmental organization with 750,000 members. Although this study provides information about only one organization, there is some reason to believe that the Sierra Club may be relatively representative of other organizations. Scholars of political organizations often regard environmental organizations as exemplary of contemporary citizen organizations.[34] The Sierra Club fits squarely into the mold of environmental movement organizations, since it was consistently a leader in the environmental movement. It was one of the ten most widely covered civic organizations in the *New York Times* and the *Washington Post* during the 1970s, 1980s, and 1990s.[35] In addition, the Sierra Club is an example of the federated organizational model typical of modern professionalized organizations.[36]

Although the Sierra Club claimed 750,000 members in 2003, fewer than 5 percent were engaged in face-to-face club activities. Only a very small percentage demonstrate more commitment than sending in a $35 membership check each year. Granted, these individuals could have joined for a range of political or personal reasons, but meaningful involvement in the Sierra Club entails becoming active in face-to-face interaction. The study focused on the 5 percent who were active in this way, and asked them what their initial goals were in becoming active. Respondents were given eight choices and told to choose their most important one: (1) enjoy/explore the outdoors, (2) influence politics and public policy to protect the environment, (3) protect natural environments, (4) meet/work with like-minded people, (5) influence public opinion, (6) become a more effective advocate/activist/leader, (7) fulfill moral/civic responsibilities, or (8) strengthen the Sierra Club. Among those eight categories, 24 percent of people chose one of the four explicitly nonpolitical goals—exploring the outdoors, meeting like-minded people, fulfilling moral/civic responsibilities, and becoming a more effective leader. Thus nearly a quarter of the Sierra Club respondents became active for recreational, social, expressive, or personal reasons.

Even more important was the finding that people who became active with nonpolitical goals were as likely to be personally committed to the Sierra Club in 2003 as people who became active for explicitly political reasons. The study asked respondents to indicate how strongly they agreed or disagreed with the following statements:

"My work in the Sierra Club influences many aspects of my life."

"I really feel as if the ExCom's problems are my problems."

"I often try to think of ways of doing my work on the ExCom more effectively."

"I feel myself to be part of the ExCom in which I work."

"What the Sierra Club stands for is very important to me."

"I am proud to tell others that I am part of the Sierra Club."

These items were combined to create a scale of personal commitment to the Sierra Club. Figure 5.1 shows the top five reasons people gave for becoming active, and the average level of personal identification with the Sierra Club for each group. It is clear that people who became active for social or recreational reasons are no less committed to the work of the Sierra Club than people who became active for explicitly political reasons.

Similar patterns hold for interview subjects in the Study of Political Pathways—they often had deep issue commitments that emerged after their initial participation. Jasmine initially got involved as a youth:

Yeah, so when I was fourteen, I was looking for a job. I actually wasn't really looking for a job. I was just walking to the store and I saw a sign that said, "Jobs for youth: fourteen and up." You know you can't get a job until you are

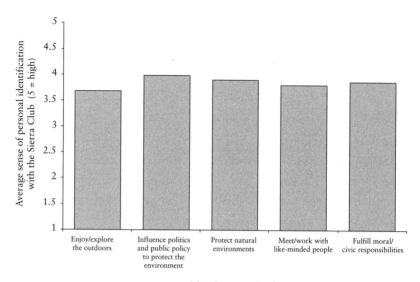

Most important goal

FIGURE 5.1. Commitment level of Executive Committee members to the Sierra Club in 2003, conditional on the motivations that first prompted them to become active. Bars represent the average level of personal identification for all respondents who listed each goal as their most important goal in becoming active. SOURCE: Data from the 2003 National Purpose, Local Action Study.

sixteen, so I came and I interviewed. I didn't know what I got myself into. I tell people that all the time—I never knew what I was getting into. I thought I was just going to watch kids or something, but I was getting paid and I didn't have anything to do after school so that was exciting. . . . So then I started working on things like sexual harassment on the streets and things like the "stop violence" campaign. . . . I didn't know the importance [of that stuff] when I first walked in the door. I never knew about that kind of stuff.

Once she got involved, she developed a deep commitment to working on issues of sexual harassment. As she put it, "I opened this can of worms." She worked with the organization she initially joined, but she also advocated for developing a sexual harassment curriculum in the public school system and carried her work beyond this initial campaign. Her work on the antiviolence campaign also expanded, and she now says, "I do care about, I do feel strongly that we focus on youth violence. That is something that really affects me personally." Many subjects described a similar trajectory, in which they initially got involved for apolitical reasons or for reasons unrelated to their current commitments. Then, getting involved with the organization opened their eyes to a cause or an injustice that needed work. As they continued to participate in activities related to this issue, they became progressively more committed to it.

Although people may join civic organizations through explicitly political events or tasks, others are drawn into the organization for alternate reasons. People join organizations for social, material, and recreational reasons. Because not all joiners are politicized prior to their participation in the organization, political organizations have the opportunity to play a role in developing motivation.

Theme 3: What Organizations Do Matters

Many subjects reported that their early experiences with public life influenced their choices to stay involved—or not. When civic and political organizations or campaigns get new volunteers, they must decide how to incorporate them into their work. The impulse may be to give volunteers the easiest task possible, such as stuffing envelopes, entering data, or making heavily scripted phone calls. Volunteers are often assigned tasks that offer little room for independent thought and are not given much responsibility for actual outcomes. A number of subjects discussed the importance of a sense of responsibility in increasing their commitment. Subjects who felt that they were delegated true responsibility were more likely to feel invested in the cause or issue for which they were working. The responsibility can be very small—the important point is that the volunteer has a sense of accountability for getting something done. Margaret, a forty-six-year-old woman active in her church, says,

One of the first times I was there . . . during this committee meeting they were talking about showing a video, like a VHS tape. They were talking about who was going to bring the soda, chips, and that sort of thing. They publicized the whole thing to the whole congregation, I think. Well, I, or maybe [name of partner], volunteered to bring the pretzels—it just seemed like the thing to do. So now we had this commitment to go. There were a lot of people there. We started going to not only services once a week but to these committee meetings monthly and maybe this movie night. And then they needed someone to bring the movie, so I did that, you know, from like Blockbuster or something. So I did that. And that was the day the whole thing became mine. It became my baby. I have now been showing these movies for fifteen years, two a year . . . [because] someone somehow asked me to bring the pretzels fifteen years ago. . . . Don't let one person bring all the snacks. If you assign it to a lot of people, they feel an obligation to show up because they feel they are important. Make a totally separate person bring the movie and another the cookies.

Margaret's motivation to stay involved came from the small bits of responsibility she was given—bringing the snacks or the movies. That eventually escalated into a larger commitment, but it began with the sense that she had a responsibility to attend the event.

For some subjects, this sense of responsibility came with a leadership role. As the member of the leadership team for her community service organization, Kelly recognizes that one element of her motivation is the feeling that she has real responsibility within the organization:

When you are actually part of the [leadership team], you have responsibility to all the people when it comes to community service. It is that sense of responsibility that gets you so involved and committed to getting stuff done for the cause and the community. . . . It makes you important. The club can't run without you, and people like to feel important, especially people who like helping the community. I think it is important to feel connected, and the more engaged you are, the more connected you feel.

Because she has true responsibility for outcomes within the organization, Kelly becomes more motivated to stay involved; she feels that she matters and that she is more connected. For both Kelly and Margaret, their organizations' decision to structure the work in particular ways had a big impact on their motivation to stay involved. With responsibility came commitment.

Explicit efforts at leadership development are one way organizations can develop commitment through responsibility. As self-governing entities, civic and political organizations are particularly dependent on their leadership to survive. Unlike leaders of other organizations whose goals are predefined, the leadership of civic and political organizations often has considerable autonomy in shaping goals.[37] Explicit efforts to recruit and develop leaders among volunteers can help them gain a greater sense of responsibility, investment, and motivation to stay involved. Subjects who participated in events or organizations with clear plans for developing future leaders indicated that such development was important to their continuing involvement. Faizah, now an advocate for immigrant rights, first got involved in public life through an ethnic organization on her college campus. She describes the importance of having people ask her to become a leader within the organization:

From my first year I showed . . . a lot of interest in being involved, so the president and vice president at the time took me under their wing and said, "You are in training." So I kind of got to see from a different perspective what it is like to run a club. . . . They really took me under their wings, and I got much more involved as a freshman.

Faizah became more committed to the cause of the organization because someone groomed her to become a leader. This theme has important implications for organizations trying to increase commitment: by delegating responsibility, by making people accountable for outcomes, and by grooming individuals for leadership positions, they can motivate people to stay involved.

Organizations can also help participants develop skills through their participation. Previous research has noted that civic organizations can help individuals develop civic skills,[38] but this research has not examined the role that learning new skills can play in increasing motivation. Several subjects noted that knowing they were learning helped them to stay involved. Jasmine initially got involved with public life when she joined a youth organizing group advocating for change in her neighborhood. She was previously not interested in politics at all and had gotten involved because she needed a job. Through this work, however, she developed a deep commitment to politics. When asked what made her stay involved, she said,

I felt like I had a role. . . . I think it is like . . . in this organization they leave it up to us and make it like our responsibility. I think I was a leader in our group. I took the role of leader in the group and took control of things. They taught us to do those things with, like, workshops and things like that. I was learning how to public speak—I had never spoken in front of a crowd—things like that.

Through her involvement, Jasmine developed new skills and gained a greater sense of responsibility.

Such learning experiences helped subjects feel empowered, increasing their motivation to stay involved. Janice describes an educational experience in which she felt treated like an equal for the first time:

(I was a student in high school [and] got a scholarship to attend the [program name] in Washington, D.C. My congressman . . . took me on a tour of the Capitol and told us all about government. That was kind of my first experience with government. It made me feel like, I guess I felt like he treated us like ordinary people, no different from anyone else. . . . When I was growing up, my family was always on the margins. . . . My dad has mental illness, and we were always on the poverty line. So getting the scholarship to go and feeling like I was just as important as the lobbyists made an impression on me.

This sense of empowerment motivated Janice to attend college in Washington, D.C., where she could be closer to the political world and re-create those feelings of empowerment.

Even for subjects from more privileged backgrounds, a sense of empowerment can come from learning. Rina grew up in a relatively privileged environment. Her parents were both professionals and were civically active in their communities. Although Rina had grown up in a household that valued participation, she was not really committed to participating until she had a personal experience that taught her she had skills she did not know she had:

Yeah, [participating in civic life] was always something I knew was the right thing to do because my parents did it, but I didn't have a personal stake in it until I went on this [backpacking] course and lived without anything except what I could carry on my back for thirty days with people that I didn't know. And I was sort of woken up to my own strength and ability to forge relationships with people that I didn't know and climb mountains. It was really an amazing experience. It was truly a defining moment in my life.

After having this experience, she committed herself to a career helping others have similar experiences and engage with their communities. Thus, learning opportunities can play an important role in helping subjects develop their motivations.

The importance of the way an organization structured work came up in several interviews. Some subjects reported initial frustration when they tried to get involved and did not really feel like their work was going anywhere or accomplishing anything. Other subjects noted that having a clear sense of what the organization's goals were—and feeling that those goals were realistic—was important in keeping them motivated. Alma discusses her involvement as a community organizer:

[It] really helped us along because we learned, not that we had unrealistic goals, but we had realistic goals and ways to get to it. . . . If you just say something like, "We want to build a youth center in [our neighborhood]," that is not going to get us anywhere. But we want a youth center with these programs in it, for the youth, because we don't have another program in the community. Okay. So we need to get funding, money, we need to associate with other organizations who want something similar, and that is how we did it. We are still a long way from it, but we are a lot closer than we were when it was just a thought.

Being able to see the strategic plan for achieving the overall goal and knowing where her work fit into that plan were important to motivating Alma to stay involved. As she worked on the smaller goals, she progressively developed more commitment to the bigger goal, the issue at stake. The choices an organization makes about how to structure the work affects the motivation of people like Alma. She needed clear goals to drive her work, and, like other subjects, she disliked situations where the short-term and long-term goals were unclear.

Organizations that enable individuals to develop social relationships with each other also appear to be more successful in motivating subjects. As demonstrated in previous research, relational concerns are always an important motivator for getting people involved. Carol, who got involved through discussions with neighbors and friends in her community, says, "It takes a little personal contact for someone like me, I guess, to become political, if that is what I am." Less research has examined the importance of ongoing social interactions in keeping people motivated to participate. Yet a number of subjects reported that participatory activities that allowed them to interact with others were more motivating than activities that were more solitary. James, a longtime environmental activist, notes that he did not have very strong commitments to the environment when he initially got involved. He had a "vague, abstract" notion that the environment was important, but he was not strongly committed to it. Once he got involved with an environmental group, however, his commitment to the issue increased.

And, you know, in the subsequent four or five years I developed a connection with a pretty close affinity group, and they pretty much became my primary social network. We all fed off one another's energy and commitment on this set of environmental values, which kind of solidified for me at that time.

James's issue commitments evolved from his interactions with other participants. This increasing issue commitment kept him involved with environmental work.

Like James, many other subjects identified social solidarity as a key factor in keeping them committed to participation. Sally, who is deeply involved with a women's group through her temple, says, "I like the women. I like the camaraderie we have. I like the feeling of sisterhood." Margaret notes that she is willing to incur greater costs to her participation in order to find this social solidarity:

You know the TV show *Cheers*? It is like the theme song—"where everybody knows your name." When you walk through the door, even if I haven't been there in a couple of months, it is the place where everybody knows your name and is glad to see you. That is why. There is a . . . congregation here in [name of hometown]. Wouldn't it be smart for me to travel five minutes instead of the forty-five minutes I do now? But I wouldn't consider it.

Margaret keeps going back to the church that is forty minutes further because she wants to be with people she knows. Male subjects reported this social aspect as being important as often as female subjects. Antonio, the immigrant rights advocate, describes why he decided to stay involved after attending one meeting of an immigration advocacy organization:

It was the first time I walked into a meeting and felt like everyone there was kind of like a friend, a brother to me. I looked up to lots of them. I just felt like I could call any of them and they would be there for me, no matter what.

Participation in public life generally requires interaction with other people, and for many, these interactions were crucial to keeping them involved. Subjects said they were more likely to stay involved when they enjoyed being with the people with whom they worked and when the organization allowed time for these relationships to develop. While social relationships emerge naturally in some cases, in other cases they can be hindered or helped by organizational choices. Rina notes that one organization in which she participated had a very positive social culture: "[The organization] has a pretty unique culture in that we take a lot of time and energy talking about where our personal lives and professional lives overlap." The ability to discuss personal issues and bring this into her participation motivated her to stay involved, whereas she had gotten burned out with other work that did not focus on the relational element. Organizations can choose to facilitate social relationships and thereby increase participants' motivation for their work.

CONCLUDING THOUGHTS

The previous chapters established the importance of personal commitments to motivating participation, particularly among underprivileged communities. The logical question that arose was where those commitments originate. What is the basis of people's personal commitments to politics? This chapter examined the pathways people take to political participation, showing how people's personal experiences shape the motivation to participate. Political motivation is not a static trait of the individual. Instead, it is a dynamic, socially constructed characteristic that grows and develops as people interact with other people and the world around them. Family and school experiences shape political motivation in youth, as do personal experiences throughout adulthood. People are not born with political motivation, in other words. They have personal experiences that may or may not bring them to politics—which may then politicize their interests.

This chapter has explored the pathways that people take toward participation in order to identify commonalities and themes. Several themes emerged. First, the choice to take action often emanated from specific personal experiences. Many people expressed abstract commitments to goals of contributing to society, but those values alone were not always enough to lead them to action. Most subjects reported having specific experiences that generated commitment to a concrete goal that inspired action. Sometimes this triggering event was political, such as a personal experience of injustice, and sometimes it was nonpolitical, such as recruitment by a friend. Second, once people made the choice to get involved, their commitment to issues often increased, causing them to stay involved. Many subjects reported first getting involved for nonpolitical reasons and then becoming more committed to political causes as a consequence of their involvement. This leads to the third theme: people who participate in political organizations are much more likely to experience increased motivation in the future—but their early experiences within the organizations can be either more motivating or less so. By paying attention to the role that organizations like political parties, campaigns, and civic associations play in developing political motivation, such organizations can better structure the experiences people have that determine how their personal concerns become politicized.

These findings have important implications for inequalities in American politics. Underlying current inequalities in representation are inequalities in participation. Remedying this begins with motivating more people to participate in politics. This chapter argues that political parties, campaigns, and civic and political associations can shape the initial experiences people have with politics and thereby affect whether or not they are motivated to participate. Unfortunately, political organizations often do not focus on building motivation but instead target and reach those who are most likely to be motivated already. As the next chapter will show, history tells us that this does not have to be so. An examination of politics in the 1890s and the 2008 election reveals a set of civic and political organizations dedicated to reaching a broad range of people. Instead of targeting narrow subsets of people for short-term mobilization, these organizations focused on mobilizing a much broader range of people for the long term (and were successful in winning electoral office). During those periods, politics in America was marked by an active citizenry that included a wide range of people.

CHAPTER 6

Looking Ahead

EVERY FOUR YEARS, Iowa moves to the forefront of political news as presidential hopefuls crawl through the state in their attempt to woo voters. Given the amount of attention showered on Iowans, a myth exists that these voters are better informed and more engaged than average American voters. Iowa voters, according to this myth, are the ideal democratic citizens, engaged seriously in the deliberative process of figuring out which candidate is their favorite candidate. Media expert Paul Waldman writes in *The American Prospect*:

And after all, we know Iowa and New Hampshire voters aren't fickle like those in some other states. They're serious and studious, applying their down-home common sense and refusing to vote for anyone unless they look them in the eye and get a sense of the person behind the politician.

Yet, as Waldman points out, the reality is that the vast majority of Iowans do not participate in the quadrennial caucuses, despite the attention given the state by presidential candidates.

If this is a typical election, somewhere between 6 and 10 percent of voting-eligible Iowans will bother to show up to a caucus. Yes, you read that right. Those vaunted Iowa voters are so concerned about the issues, so involved in the political process, so serious about their solemn deliberative responsibilities as guardians of the first-in-the-nation contest, that nine out of ten can't manage to haul their butts down to the junior high on caucus night. One might protest that caucusing is hard—it requires hours of time and a complicated sequence of standing in corners, raising hands, and trading votes. . . . But so what? If ten presidential candidates personally came to your house to beg for your vote, wouldn't you set aside an evening when decision time finally came?[1]

Despite numerous opportunities to meet presidential candidates in small settings, despite multiple calls from various campaigns seeking to recruit votes, and despite endless media attention on the political activities in the state, most Iowans cannot be bothered to give up a few hours every four years to participate in the their state's caucuses. The media hailed record-breaking turnout in the 2008 Iowa caucuses, when Barack Obama and Hillary Clinton vied for the Democratic nomination, and John McCain, Rudy Giuliani, Mike Huckabee, and Mitt Romney fought for the Republican nomination. Yet, even in this hotly contested race, only 16.3 percent of eligible voters in Iowa turned out to vote.[2]

The Iowa caucuses thus encapsulate a simple truth about politics: getting people to participate is hard. This truth is the challenge at the center of this book. How can we get more people to participate in politics? In particular, how can we engage people who are traditionally marginalized in our political system? Despite years of fruitful research on the factors that facilitate political participation, we still struggle to bring poorer, less educated people into politics. As pointed out in the introduction, the gap in participation between people with high and low levels of education has only increased in the past several decades. To broaden participation, we need a better understanding of the mechanisms that engage traditionally marginalized individuals in politics.

This book focuses on mechanisms that encourage participation among underrepresented groups. Participation is fundamental to democratic citizenship because people who participate are more likely to have their views represented. Disparities in participation are thus at the root of disparities in representation, or inequality, in American politics. The existence of inequality in American politics is unlikely to surprise very many political observers. Prominent scholars have documented the tendency of policy makers to preferentially weigh the opinions of wealthy individuals.[3] Journalists frequently depict images of lobbyists making backroom deals with policy makers. Many citizens believe that "other" people are more likely to influence politics than they are. Inequality is a durable, but unfortunate, reality in American politics. Fixing it depends on fixing inequalities in participation. If people who lack financial, educational, or civic resources do not participate in politics, then these inequalities in representation are unlikely to disappear.

The issue public hypothesis represents one way of bringing people of low education, income, and other resources into politics. There are many ways to engage people in the political system, and for different people at different times, different factors will be most important. This book argues that motivation is particularly important for facilitating participation among traditionally marginalized people. People who have few of the resources necessary for participation must really *want* to participate. Only then will they overcome the hurdles to participation. What makes someone want to participate in politics? This book examines how personal commitments to issues can motivate people to participate. People who belong to issue publics on particular issues are more likely to be active on those issues. Recognizing how issue public membership facilitates participation thus highlights one way of bringing traditionally marginalized individuals into the political process.

THE ISSUE PUBLIC HYPOTHESIS

The issue public hypothesis begins with a puzzle posed in Chapter 1. Most of the research on participation has argued that people need both motivation and resources to get involved (both of which can emerge through recruitment). People must want to get involved and must be capable of doing so. According to traditional models of participation, being motivated means being generally interested in, knowledgeable about, and efficacious with regard to politics. People with those traits are more likely to have the educational, financial, and civic resources necessary for participation. Yet history has shown multiple examples of people who do not have high levels of political interest, knowledge, and efficacy but nonetheless get involved. What motivates this group of people to become involved in political life?

At the center of the issue public hypothesis is the notion that people are motivated by their personal goals. Previous empirical analyses of political participation have given only limited attention to personal goals in examining motivation and have assumed that people must be politicized prior to participation. Chapter 2 delineated an approach to understanding motivation that drew on psychological research on motivation and argued that people will get involved if they recognize politics as a way of fulfilling their personal goals, regardless of how generally interested in politics they are. This approach moves away from focusing only on static traits related to a person's potential to get involved and instead examines whether the person has made connections and has personal commitments that can motivate participation. Some people get involved because political interests beckon them to do so; others get involved because personal concerns move them to take political action.

Depending on how we conceptualize motivation, political participation can appear to be something that many people want to do or that only a few people want to do. Chapter 3 delineated two conceptions of how political motivation is distributed in the population. While the attentive public hypothesis argues that only a small group of elites are politically interested and aware, the issue public hypothesis asserts that many people are interested in politics, but primarily around the issues they care personally about. People choose which issues are most important to them—if any— and focus their time and energy becoming informed and active regarding those issues. These people may not appear to be very politically motivated when asked general questions about politics, but they are motivated by their specific issue of concern. Because many different people can be engaged on many different issues, the issue public hypothesis argues that political motivation is distributed more broadly in the population than the attentive public hypothesis assumes. Acknowledging that people will put the most energy and attention toward the issues they care most about, in other words, allows for a much broader array of people to be politically motivated than we may have originally thought. The data in Chapter 3 showed that belonging to an issue public is not limited to people who are wealthy or well educated. Instead, people of all kinds of backgrounds have political issues that are personally important to them.

The question then becomes whether belonging to an issue public has any impact on participation. Chapter 4 showed that people with strong personal commitments to politics are more likely to participate. The question of who participates in politics is an old question, but Chapter 4 took a fresh look by focusing on personal commitments. Existing models of participation often focus more on the factors that *enable* participation (such as civic resources and skills, recruitment, and so on) than on the factors that *motivate* participation. Previous research on political participation has acknowledged the importance of motivation in facilitating participation but has conceptualized motivation only as generalized levels of political interest, knowledge, and efficacy. This ignores the many people who are not generally engaged in politics but are engaged on particular policy issues. By examining the impact that belonging to an issue public has on participation, Chapter 4 showed that people with strong personal commitments to policy are more likely to participate.

Analyses in Chapter 4 also showed that belonging to an issue public is particularly important in explaining participation among people who do not have many of the resources assumed necessary for participation. People from all backgrounds will be more likely to participate if they have the necessary resources, such as time, knowledge about how the political system works, information about politics, and civic skills. In addition, people of all backgrounds will be more likely to participate if they are asked to do so. For people with few financial, educational, and civic resources, however, motivation becomes especially important. Like the Katrina refugees discussed in Chapter 1, these people have considerable hurdles to overcome in participation. Finding the time and information they need to vote or to volunteer for a political cause is no easy task. To overcome such hurdles, people of underresourced backgrounds must be highly motivated. Belonging to an issue public is one way in which they may be highly motivated. Understanding that issue public membership facilitates participation is thus particularly important for increasing participation among people without much money or education.

The importance of issue public membership to participation and democratic representation raises the question of where this kind of political motivation originates. How do people's commitments to policy arise? Previous research shows that issue public membership is multiply determined and that many types of life events and personal experiences can generate strong personal commitment to a political issue. The question is whether there are any commonalities or patterns to the ways people get involved. Chapter 5 examined the pathways people take to participation and explored three clear themes that emerged across interviews with subjects in the Study of Political Pathways. First, people often need a specific triggering experience to activate their involvement, regardless of the broad values they may express. For instance, many people believe that getting involved is important, but they still do not participate. Those who do get involved can often identify a specific event, experience, or person that pushed them to take action. Second, people's issue commitments often grow out of their participation. They often first get involved for alternate reasons, such as a desire to meet other people. Once they do get involved, however, their commitment to a political issue deepens. Third, the choice to get involved and to stay involved in politics often depends on what organizations or campaigns did. Having a clear set of goals for participation motivates individuals to stay involved. Having more responsibility gives individuals a sense that their contributions are worthwhile, and they are then more likely to stay involved. Explicit leadership development efforts motivate individuals to increase their level of involvement. Social and relational opportunities are often important for increasing subjects' motivation. Characteristics of how the organization or campaign structured its work, developed relationships among participants, and instilled a sense of hope in participants facilitate—or depress— peoples' commitment to participating.

Taken together, these themes imply that political organizations can play a crucial role in developing issue public members because the choice to get involved is the product of an individual's life experiences. People may have values that create general interest in politics or a commitment to public service, but most people need a triggering experience to act on those values. What people do, who they meet, and what they experience affect how much desire they have to participate in the political system and whether they develop personal issue commitments. The social aspect of political motivation provides political organizations with enormous opportunities to motivate participation.

POLITICAL ORGANIZATIONS
AND POLITICAL MOTIVATION

In observing nineteenth-century America, Alexis de Tocqueville famously marveled at the range of associations he witnessed. "Association is the mother of all forms of democracy," he wrote. The strength of America's democratic culture, he asserted, was in the propensity of Americans to join together to achieve collective goals. These institutions of democracy may play a key role in generating the desire to participate. The findings in this book imply that what organizations—such as local party organizations or citizen-based interest groups—do, in terms of how they structure people's experiences of participation in politics, may encourage (or neglect) the development of political engagement. Although some political observers may be skeptical that political organizations can engage the broad swaths of apathetic citizens in American politics, history shows that more people can be engaged than are engaged now. An examination of political organizing in the late nineteenth century and in Barack Obama's 2008 presidential campaign provides evidence consistent with the idea that organizations can become a mechanism by which people's personal experiences become politicized. Further, organizations may have the potential to systematically encourage motivation. Instead of relying on episodic, biographical experiences to motivate people, political organizations can play a key role in encouraging political engagement.

The skeptic's response to the notion that political organizations can engage broad groups of people to get involved in politics is that dominant trends in current politics point in the opposite direction. Until Obama's presidential campaign in 2008, it seemed unlikely that political organizations would engage previously disengaged voters in politics given the current focus on activation through microtargeting in political campaigns. In the 2004 election the Democratic Party relied heavily on the guidance of "Demzilla" to launch extensive get-out-the-vote (GOTV) efforts. Neither a seasoned campaign operative nor a wise sage of democratic politics, Demzilla was a computer—a computer with a giant database of voter profiles. The Republicans had one too—the "GOP Voter Vault." Both parties mined their data carefully to decide who was most likely to be a successful recruit and how to tailor the party message to particular groups of voters. With basic demographic information about individuals, as well as extra tidbits such as what kind of car they drove, how many long-distance phone calls they made, and how often they had voted in the past, Demzilla could tell Democratic campaign staff if people were likely to vote and, if so, what issues they cared most about. If someone turned out to be an "Education First" voter, then the Democrats would try to send a teacher to the person's home armed with talking points about the negative effects of President George W. Bush's No Child Left Behind policies.[4]

This mode of voter activation has increasingly become the norm in American politics. In his book *By Invitation Only: The Rise of Exclusive Politics in the United States*, Steven Schier distinguishes between democratic mobilization and activation.[5] Whereas democratic mobilization involves broad-based outreach to citizens in an attempt to foster long-term engagement with politics, activation focuses on energizing latent tendencies toward participation within specific groups of citizens. Activation is about turning people out in the short term. Schier argues that the decline of political parties, the increasing number of interest groups, and the emergence of new communications technology in the latter decades of the twentieth century prompted a shift from democratic mobilization to activation. Thus, since the 1970s, activation has increasingly replaced mobilization in American political campaigns.[6]

Some argue that activation politics has fragmented the base of people participating in democratic life. On the one hand, targeting through Demzilla and the GOP Voter Vault offers enormous possibilities to parties, candidates, and other organizations seeking to mobilize voters. Targeting enables campaigns to deploy their resources effectively, in directions that are most likely to turn out voters. This approach to politics is built on consumer marketing. Through careful research, companies figure out what consumers want—perhaps even before consumers actually want it—and then create products designed specifically to meet those desires. As targeting technology becomes more sophisticated, organizations can make more specific appeals grounded in informed guesses about which potential voters will give them the most "bang for their buck." Thus, a well-educated lawyer who shops at Whole Foods and donates regularly to his church is likely to receive invitations to political events, phone calls to join campaigns, and reminders to vote. Some political observers have asserted that such sophisticated targeting efforts have the potential to change the kind of democracy we live in. These methods of activation result in market fragmentation. As Alex Gage, president of TargetPoint, a leading microtargeting company, says, "It's market segmentation. We're separating which voters are the most profitable, then finding what it is they like about my product. In this case, my candidate."[7] The result is an ongoing process of differentiation, division, and exclusion. As Christopher Hunter, an expert on political technology says, the activation model of participation creates "little bubbles around people" with targeted messaging that limits opportunities for broader public dialogues.[8]

Data on recruitment by recent political campaigns buttresses the notion that activation models of participation reinforce existing political inequalities. Because outreach is concentrated on people most likely to vote for a given candidate, campaigns are more likely to neglect people who have not voted in the past—such as poorer, less educated, and more mobile people. For instance, in 2000 and 2004, the parties were more likely to activate wealthy, well-educated people with high levels of general interest in politics. Drawing on data from the ANES, Figure 6.1 shows the average education, household income, and general political interest of people recruited by political parties in the 2000 and 2004 general elections. Clearly, people who were recruited were likely to have above-average levels of education, income, and interest—whereas people who were not recruited were likely to have below-average levels of education, income,

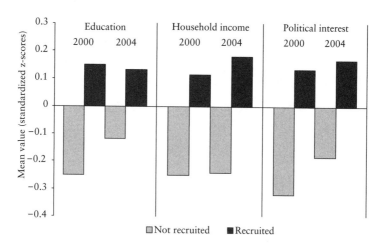

FIGURE 6.1. Average education, income, and political interest of people who were recruited and not recruited by political parties, 2000 and 2004. Bars represent the mean value for each group, calculated as standardized z-scores. SOURCE: Data from the 2000 and 2004 ANES cross-sectional studies.

and interest.[9] Political campaigns in 2000 and 2004 reached out to people who had already reaped the advantages of the political system—wealthy, well-educated voters who were relatively easy to activate for participation. These were the people likely to have the resources necessary for participation. As previous research shows, these disproportionate levels of recruitment by political parties among more advantaged citizens also compound the likelihood that these advantaged citizens will exercise a disproportionate voice in politics.

Historically, there is evidence that political parties and civic associations have engaged a much broader populace in interpersonal activity.[10] An examination of patterns of mobilization in the 1890s and in Barack Obama's 2008 presidential campaign, for example, demonstrates that parties and political clubs can target broad groups of citizens to build their coalitions. Instead of activating only the most motivated individuals, campaigns in these two instances mobilized citizens across the demographic and social spectrum.

Politics in the last two decades of the nineteenth century provides one example of the ways in which democratic organizations can organize broad swaths of the population. Federated civic associations played a crucial role in organizing the American public during this time.[11] Associations like the Odd Fellows and the Elks had national, state, and local bodies that organized people across class lines and provided a means for them to connect to others and to a broader political system.[12] Historian Mark Kornbluh argues that this was the last period of intense participation in American politics.[13] Notably, participation during this period not only was widespread but bridged traditional social and demographic gaps. In his history of mass participation, Kornbluh argues that "voting was nearly universal among those who were enfranchised."[14] M. Ostrogorski observed that political parades represented people of all social groupings, "from the prince of finance" down to the common laborer.[15] Managers and laborers, urbanites and agrarians, immigrants and nativists, could all take part in the common experience of political campaigns. Although they might not agree, they could all find a way to get involved.

Parties and political organizations played a crucial role in making this happen. The local party organizations were particularly important in "[bringing] electoral politics to the American public and [leading] a partisan electorate to the ballot box in unprecedented numbers."[16] Michael McGerr attributes parties' success to their individual style of mobilization through local organizations.[17] During this period, extended periods of campaigning and social events surrounded frequent local elections:

Each presidential campaign is the signal for an outburst of clubs, Republican and Democratic, of commercial travelers, of clerks of dry-goods stores, of lawyers, or merchants, of railroad employees, of workmen's clubs formed, not by wards, but by workshop, the workmen in a large factory dividing, perhaps into two clubs, the one Republican, the other Democratic; clubs of coloured men; Irish, German, Polish, Swedish clubs; even Republican or Democratic "cyclists" brigades.[18]

Local political clubs regarded mobilization of their electorate as their responsibility. The goal of the clubs was to address the particular concerns of constituents and to create connections between individuals and the organization.[19] These clubs organized people in part by providing "spectacle" and entertainment. Electoral politics provided "free recreation" to people, a "sense of fellowship" (particularly for men), and "connections between isolated localities."[20] By embedding politics in the social lives of voters, parties and civic associations were able to achieve widespread mobilization. The basis of participation in parties and civic associations was broader than just politics or policy issues—it encompassed people's social, recreational, and relational goals as well.

Much previous research on mobilization in this period has assumed that parties were effective because they could rely on "material" incentives to organize voters. In a historical examination of party activists, Joseph Schlesinger notes the prominence of "office-seekers," who work for the party to obtain political office, and "benefit-seekers," who derive benefits indirectly from their party's control of office.[21] Multiple scholars have argued that, until the 1960s, party activists and the party rank-and-file were dominated by benefit-seekers who primarily sought patronage and were relatively devoid of "ideological fervor."[22] People participated because they got jobs or other material benefits from participation. These scholars argue that parties' ability to mobilize large swaths of voters diminished as patronage systems declined and parties no longer relied on selective material incentives to engage voters.

A feature of these material incentives that has not been highlighted much in previous research is that they were most effective when they were personalized. Parties during the populist era were not successful in organizing farmers until they coupled the material incentives embedded in policy with material incentives that had a more direct impact on the personal lives of farmers. In his history of the populist movement, Lawrence Goodwyn argues that the development of the movement depended on finding organizing techniques that did not depend on appealing to the political outrage of farmers.[23] Farmers had been increasingly marginalized economically for decades in the nineteenth century, and several organizations had attempted to organize them into a coherent political movement. These organizations relied on political appeals that highlighted the material gains farmers could derive by supporting policies of the Populist Party. Without grounding these material incentives in the personal lives of farmers, these organizations repeatedly failed because they were unable to sustain widespread mobilization of farmers—despite the economic and political unease of farmers: "Though reformers tended to blame the 'apathy' and 'near-sightedness' of the people, their problem essentially was one of simple organization: they needed to find an effective instrument of recruitment. Stump speeches based on complicated greenback monetary arguments were simply not enough to affect the way people acted politically."[24] Farmers needed a more personal appeal to bring them into the organization.

It was not until the National Farmers' Alliance created the first large-scale working-class cooperative that farmers truly came together. This approach to mobilizing is based on a system of "selective incentives" common to many interest groups. By offering members a range of non-political incentives—such as the hotel discounts that AARP offers or the paraphernalia that groups like the Sierra Club offer—interest groups induce membership in a way much like that used by the National Farmers' Alliance.[25] Farmers flocked to the alliance not because of its political goals but because of the economic possibilities embodied in the cooperative. By bringing farmers together to sell crops at higher prices, obtain basic agricultural supplies at lower prices, and thereby alleviate some of the economic anxiety of farmers, the alliance was the first organization to unite farmers successfully under one banner. Goodwyn observes, "The reality that explained the remarkable organizing potential of the Alliance cooperative rested in the substance of the daily lives of millions of farmers."[26] Farmers joined the alliance not because lofty political goals appealed to them but because they had daily economic woes the cooperative could help solve.

The key difference between the alliance and modern-day interest groups, however, is that the alliance intentionally built on the connections initiated by the cooperative to further politicize its members. This contrasts with modern organizations that usually put their members on a mailing list but rarely engage them in face-to-face interaction.[27] Limited by technology, the alliance had no choice but to engage in interpersonal interaction. Leaders organized a group of lecturers to go into local cooperatives across the nation to make the connections between farmers' economic concerns and political events. Although farmers did not join the cooperative for political reasons, they became politicized through it.

The . . . experiences of millions of farmers within their cooperatives proceeded to "educate" them about the prevailing forms of economic power and privilege in America. This process of education was . . . elaborated through a far-flung agency of internal communication, the 40,000 lecturers of the Alliance lecturing system. . . . [A]fter the effort of the Alliance at economic self-help had been defeated by the financial and political institutions of industrial America, the people of the movement turned to independent political action by creating their own institution, the People's Party. All of these experiences . . . may be seen as an evolutionary pattern of democratic organizing that generated, and in turn was generated by, an increasing self-awareness on the part of the participants.[28]

To farmers, politics was almost an accidental by-product of their membership in the cooperative. By consciously building on the relationships created by the cooperative, however, and building connections between farmers' personal concerns and politics, the alliance successfully created a sense of group consciousness among the farmers—a consciousness that became the basis of the populist political movement in the late nineteenth century.

This account of the origins of the populist movement is consistent with the findings of the Study of Political Pathways. Subjects in that study often reported first joining an organization for nonpolitical reasons, whether social (wanting to find like-minded people) or instrumental (wanting to find a better school for their kids). Their subsequent experience within the organization affected whether or not they became more interested in the political aspects of the organization. Any subsequent political activity, however, was inextricably linked to the personal goals that first brought them to the organization. For the alliance and for the organizations in the Study of Political Pathways, recognition of the personal sources of political motivation mattered. By embedding politics in the daily lives of farmers and citizens, parties and political organizations in the late nineteenth century successfully mobilized a broader swath of the population than ever before. People across multiple socioeconomic and social boundaries participated in politics as parties and local clubs made politics a source of daily entertainment. People may have come to these parades, meetings, and clubs for a wide range of reasons—including material reasons—but parties and political organizations ultimately found success by linking personal concerns to political activity.

The historic presidential campaign of Barack Obama provides a more modern example of the way political organizations can make this link between personal concerns and political activity. The Obama campaign relied more on grassroots organizing than most campaigns have in the past.[29] Pundits have credited this organizing strategy with helping Obama win key victories during the Democratic primary season to defeat Hillary Clinton for the party's nomination.[30] Yet, in 2008, the Obama campaign could not rely on the same kind of selective material incentives that party leaders in the 1890s could. The campaign was nonetheless successful in tying politics to people's personal lives. The training that the Obama campaign gave to organizers around the country emphasized reaching out to people based on their own personal motivations. These motivations, articulated as personal stories, expressed both material and nonmaterial goals. The training "encourage[d] volunteers to share their own life stories with voters, in the belief that by speaking from the heart, they [would] turn the tedious—phone-banking, door-knocking—into a communal mission."[31] As Buffy Wicks, a field director for the campaign, said, "What we want you to do is tell people your story. Tell them why you want Barack Obama to be president."[32] One of the subjects in the Study of Political Pathways described it as follows:

It is talking to the heart of what people believe in. . . . You don't have to say much. All you have to do is start [asking] people what do they think about what is going on. You don't even have to know anything about politics. . . . All you have to do is talk about what is happening today . . . what they feel in the streets . . . whatever it is, talk to them about those kinds of things, and they start getting fired up. . . . And then I talk about me and where I'm from, what I'm doing, my dad, black people, life, death, education, and more importantly . . . I'm now a guy running my own business with no basic health [insurance]. I tried to get to health benefits with a preexisting condition—it's like $800 a month . . . but I can't pay that. And that's my story. And then I talk about how this fits into Barack Obama and how he can effect change in your own life. . . . [If] they think this black man isn't going to change things all of a sudden, I say, "Excuse me, what are we doing here? We have already changed everything. The fact that you and I are talking on the telephone is already changing everything."

The campaign trained its organizers to talk to people about the personal stories and issues that motivated them. These stories may express a range of hopes, from the desire to obtain health insurance to the desire to elect an African-American candidate. By telling their own stories, organizers showed others how to make the connection between their personal lives and the Obama campaign. Relying on this strategy of personal connections, the Obama campaign has been more successful in engaging groups of people who previously were not engaged in the political process—minorities, young voters, and people from low-income backgrounds.[33]

Studying these instances of widespread mobilization in the 1890s and 2008 demonstrates the key role that parties and political organizations can play in mobilizing voters. Most modern political organizations are not motivating as broad a democratic base as they could because they assume that motivating people to participate in politics is too hard (or perhaps impossible). This assumption undergirds the tendency of political institutions to target those who already participate (or are already likely to participate) for mobilization. The populist movement in the 1890s and the Obama campaign in 2008 took a different approach that recognized the personal bases of political motivation. These organizations thus reached out to people through their personal concerns, then subsequently brought them into the political process. Not only was it entirely feasible for parties and political organizations to mobilize a broad base of voters in the 1890s, but it was the norm. Changes in structural incentives in the twentieth century have eroded this system of politics, such that widespread mobilization of voters may seem less likely now then ever before.[34] Through its strategy of organizing around personal stories, however, the Obama campaign presents a model for applying broad-based mobilization tactics in modern politics.

IMPLICATIONS FOR RESEARCH

More research is necessary before we can fully understand the role of political organizations in motivating participation. This book renews a focus on the individual values and commitments that people bring to politics. Often researchers ignore the rich complex of motivations and concerns that any individual brings to politics. These are hard to measure in a reliable way and are often difficult to pin down conceptually as well. Nevertheless, the research described here has shown that knowing what people care about matters. It matters because it helps explain patterns of political participation. Given the importance of personal policy commitments in the democratic process, more scholarship examining the life experiences and micro-level factors that can help an individual develop personal policy commitments is warranted.

Most research on political participation and democratic representation has focused on the population as a whole to determine the factors that relate to higher levels of participation and representation. I have argued that focusing more specifically on certain subgroups of people may yield valuable insights that could help ameliorate inequalities in American politics. Different factors will be more important for different kinds of people. More research is needed on mechanisms that could politically engage people who have few educational, financial, and civic resources. The analyses in earlier chapters showed that people with strong personal commitments to politics are more likely to participate, regardless of their wealth or education level. But are there other ways to engage traditionally marginalized groups of people in politics? This book has begun to explore ways that political institutions can shape participation by shaping people's motivation. Are there other ways institutions can facilitate participation among different groups of people? Conducting more research that acknowledges this possibility and examines the forces that are most important for engaging underrepresented people can lay the foundation for a broader democracy.

In addition, there is work to be done on the role that political organizations can play in affecting the motivations of citizens. The relationships between issue publics and political outcomes are not static. Instead, issue publics exist in a dynamic equilibrium with elected officials, political institutions, and other members of the mass public. Changes to the structure and behavior of one can potentially affect behavior in the other. Elucidating the relationship between issue publics and political institutions can highlight the mechanisms through which issue publics develop (for instance, how do interest groups develop personal policy commitments?), as well as the way their preferences are expressed in the political system (for example, do their preferences—or their participatory activity—have to be aggregated to have an impact?). Highlighting, studying, and understanding these commitments, then, can help us enhance the role of issue publics in the political system.

Future research can address important limitations to this study. First and foremost, the data used in this book are not ideal for testing these hypotheses. An ideal dataset would have multiple indicators of issue public membership and would contain more nuanced data on the factors that influence participation. Time series data on issue publics and participation could improve the causal analyses in Chapter 4. Second, this study is only the first of many analyses that could be done to refine the issue public hypothesis. This book focuses on developing and testing the idea that issue public membership affects political participation, but a broader study with more data could examine this hypothesis alongside other competing hypotheses. What else can motivate participation? How does issue public motivation compare? How do issue publics affect democratic representation? Third, this study relies on observational data. To confirm a causal relationship between issue publics and participation or between political organizations and motivation, experimental studies are necessary.

Despite these limitations, this study has used the best available data to take the first step in understanding the relationship between personal commitments and participation. In doing so, it extends previous research on issue publics, which looked only at how issue public membership affects certain behaviors, but not how it affects political participation. In addition, it deepens our understanding of who participates and, in particular, the mechanisms that motivate people from traditionally marginalized backgrounds to participate. The results of this study thus lay the foundation for a future research agenda that looks more carefully at other dimensions of the relationship between personal motivations and democratic politics.

IMPLICATIONS FOR POLITICAL REFORM

This book has explored the relationship between varying levels of personal concern for public policy issues and participation. Because different people care about different issues, people will connect to and participate in the political system in different ways. Previous research on the importance of participation for democratic representation indicates that differences in participation affect who is represented on any given policy issue. The question of who is represented is central to any democracy. Whose voices are heard in the policy-making process? Who influences government decisions? Democratic governments, by definition, should be responsive to the will of the people, yet most democracies privilege certain people over others. Certain people are better represented. Despite the significance of this issue to American democracy, there is surprisingly little systematic empirical work on the question of who is represented. The idea that wealthy people are better represented than poorer people is often bandied about, but it is only very recently that the idea has been systematically tested. In examining the impact of issue publics on participation, the present study proposes an alternative account of who may be represented.

What are the possibilities for reform implied by this study? In seeking to remedy inequality in American politics, many reformers call for a broadening of participation in politics.[35] Traditional models of participation maintain that the best way to accomplish this is by making it easier for people to participate. For years, we have understood that people are more likely to participate in politics when the benefits of participation outweigh the costs.[36] For several decades, reformers have tried to reduce the costs of participation by making it easier for people to participate. The Great Society reforms of the late 1960s and early 1970s sought to open political institutions to "maximum feasible participation." Both Democrats and Republicans instituted reforms in the early 1970s designed to make it easier for the "ordinary voter" to have a part in the presidential nominating process. Television and the Internet have made it much easier for citizens to find information about political candidates and the political process. The landmark National Voter Registration Act of 1993—popularly known as the Motor Voter Act—streamlined the voter registration process by allowing for mail-in registration, providing people with forms at their Department of Motor Vehicles, and otherwise making it simpler for people to vote. Additionally, by the time of the 2006 election, thirty-five states were allowing for some form of early voting.[37] According to the League of Women Voters, a leading advocate for government reform, many of these reforms were instituted to bring "added convenience to the voting process" and to "boost participation . . . while making voting less of a hassle for one and all."[38]

Unfortunately, although the costs of participation have been declining for decades now, rates of participation among marginalized groups have not increased. Clearly, simply making it easier to participate is not enough to bring traditionally marginalized individuals into politics. The question, thus, is how to bring people at different levels of education (and other resources) into politics. The findings of this study imply that the key to broadening participation is not in making it easier to participate but in making it more *worthwhile* to participate. One way of bringing people of limited resources into politics is to make them want to participate. People who have strong personal commitments to politics are more likely to participate and have their voices heard. How can more personal commitments to politics be generated?

Engendering the motivation to participate is hard because the sources of motivation can be dependent on individual, biographical experiences. Ordinary citizens often find the desire to participate in politics embedded in their everyday experiences. Frequently, people conceive of politics as being distant from their daily lives, a concern far removed from—and often in competition with—the rigors of family, work, and personal relationships. Indeed, the Founding Fathers encouraged this with their image of the politician as an individual removed from the "passions" of daily existence, able to render distant and thereby impartial judgments. This image fostered the notion that democracy happens far away from the mundane details of people's lives. The truth is, however, that politics is embedded inextricably in people's lives. The desire to participate arises not from attachment to a distant goal but instead from attachment to everyday concerns. Only by building connections between politics and these everyday concerns do people gain the emotional attachments necessary for motivation.

The connection of political motivation to people's everyday lives highlights the importance of personal and interpersonal life experiences in shaping the desire to participate. People are not born with a desire to participate or not to participate. Instead, their desire emerges organically from their life experiences. This implies that motivation changes. It is not static or predetermined in any way. Instead, it shifts and develops over the short and the long term. This aspect of motivation also implies that people's social relationships are key to structuring their desire to participate. Only in dialogue with others do people realize and articulate the connection between their personal lives and politics. Two people with the same experiences may not be motivated to participate in the same way if they have not fit politics into their own narratives about life.

One approach to systematically facilitating motivation, then, is to structure the kind of social experiences people have in politics. Political organizations have the potential to play a key role here. Historically, they have been important in building and sustaining the motivation to participate in citizens. More research is necessary here. Demonstrating the independent effect of organizational activity on political motivation is no easy task, and the analyses presented here are just a beginning. Further analyses are necessary to ascertain what impact organizations have and how they have that impact. How can organizations change an individual's level of political motivation? And further, how much can they change that motivation? What kinds of practices are most likely to engage a broader group of people in the political system?

Questions such as these are linked to a long tradition of research on the ways political institutions can shape individual political behavior. Democracy is not only about responsiveness but also about creating capacity in citizens. Alexis de Tocqueville observed this in nineteenth-century America, noting the way in which pervasive local civic associations acted as "schools of democracy." These associations taught citizens about public engagement, developed the civic skills necessary for political action, and endowed citizens with the motivation to be involved in politics. In other words, democratic organizations taught individuals to be democratic citizens. Although research and reform in this area has dropped off in recent years, this study lays the foundation for refocusing on the importance of personal motivations and the role political organizations can play in motivating people to participate in politics.

REFERENCE MATTER

Issue Public Measures from the 1980, 1984, 1996, 2000, and 2004 American National Election Studies

Questions assessing issue public membership in each of the cross-sectional studies of the American National Election Studies (ANES) read as follows:

1980: "Using the blue card [an ANES 100-point thermometer], tell me: how important is it to you that the government (continue/change) what it is doing so that it (stays close/comes closer) to your own position on this issue?" The variable was recoded such that only respondents who answered "100" were coded as being in the issue public. The issues included on this survey were government aid to minorities, government services versus spending, defense spending, government action on inflation versus unemployment, government support for jobs and a standard of living versus letting people get ahead on their own, women's equality, U.S. policy toward Russia, and abortion.

1984: "How important is it to you that the federal government do what you think is best on this issue of XXX?" 4 = Extremely important; 3 = Very important; 2 = Somewhat important; 1 = Not important at all. Issue public members were coded as those who answered "Extremely important." The issues included on this survey were government services versus spending, government support for jobs and a standard of living versus letting people get ahead on their own, women's equality, and U.S. policy toward Central America.

The 1996, 2000, and 2004 surveys all asked the question as follows: "How important is this issue to you personally?" 4 = Extremely important; 3 = Very important; 2 = Somewhat important; 1 = Not too important; 0 = Not important at all. Issue public members were coded as those who answered "Extremely important."

- In 1996 the issues included on the survey were government aid to minorities, government services versus spending, defense spending, protecting the environment versus protecting jobs and a standard of living, and abortion.
- In 2000 the issues included on the survey were toughening environmental regulations, gun control, and abortion.
- In 2004 the issues included on the survey were government aid to blacks, government aid to Hispanics, government services versus spending, defense spending, government support for jobs and a standard of living versus letting people get ahead on their own, women's equality, gun control, and abortion.

Comparison of Variables from the 1990 American Citizen Participation Study and the 1996 American National Election Study

The list below describes the way each variable was measured in the 1990 American Citizen Participation Study (CPS) and the 1996 American National Election Study (ANES). These variables were used primarily in the analyses in Chapter 4.

DEPENDENT VARIABLE: OVERALL ACTIVITY INDEX

- CPS: Constructed as an additive scale of dichotomous variables indicating participation in the following activities: voting, campaign work, contributing campaign money, membership in a political organization, writing a letter to an official, trying to persuade someone how to vote, and attending a political meeting or rally. Scale ranges from zero to 8.
- ANES: Constructed as an additive scale from dichotomous variables for participation in the following activities: voting in the 1996 election; spending time volunteering in the past year; being involved with a group in which the respondent discusses politics; talking to others to persuade them to vote for/against a party or candidate; working with others or joining an organization to work on a community problem; attending meetings, speeches, or rallies for the candidate; contributing money to a political candidate or cause; and working for any one of the parties or candidates. Scale ranges from zero to 8.

RESOURCES

- Education
  - CPS: Education coded into six categories based on the highest level of education completed by the respondent: grammar school and less, some high school, high school graduate/GED, some college, college graduate, postgraduate work. Scale ranges from 1 to 6.
  - ANES: Coded as a 7-point scale: 1 = 8 grades or less and no diploma or equivalent; 2 = 9–11 grades, no further schooling; 3 = High school diploma or GED; 4 = More than 12 years of schooling but no degree; 5 = Junior or community college–level degree; 6 = BA-level degrees; 17+ years, no postgraduate work; 7 = Advanced degree, including LLB. Scale ranges from 1 to 7.

- Vocabulary
  - CPS: Sum of the number of correct answers the respondent provided to ten vocabulary questions. Scale ranges from zero to 10.
  - ANES: Not included in analysis.

- Family income
  - CPS: Income coded into six levels: under 15K, 15–35K, 35–50K, 50–75K, 75–125K, over 125K. Scale ranges from 1 to 6, with higher numbers indicating more income.
  - ANES: Income coded into six levels: under 15K, 15–35K, 35–50K, 50–75K, 75–105K, over 105K. Scale ranges from 1 to 6, with higher numbers indicating more income.
- Civic skills
  - CPS: Opportunities to practice civic skills in three domains: job, organizations, and church. Within each institution, respondents were asked if they had to do any of the following four activities: write a letter, attend to a meeting where they take part in making decisions, plan or chair a meeting, or give a presentation or speech. Responses were given one point for each activity they did in each institution, and responses are added to create a total measure of civic skills. Variable ranges from zero to 12.
  - ANES: Scale calculated by adding dichotomous variables indicating whether the respondent is active in a range of nineteen different organizations and church groups. Activity questions asked as "In the last 12 months have you taken part in any activities sponsored by this group or attended a meeting of this group?" Scale ranges from zero to 19.
- Free time
  - CPS: Measured based on a series of questions about the time spent by the respondent on four types of activities in an average day: work/employment, study, sleep, home and family activities. Free time is calculated as the time remaining after necessary activities are subtracted from 24 hours. Variable ranges from zero to 20.
  - ANES: Not included in analysis.

RECRUITMENT

- CPS: Coded as an additive scale for whether or not the respondent was asked to work for a government official, take part in a protest, or take part in local community work, and the number of times the respondent was asked to work for or contribute to a campaign or candidate. Scale ranges from zero to 5.
- ANES: Coded as an additive scale for whether or not the respondent was contacted by a party, another group, or a religious or moral group about the campaign or candidate. Scale ranges from zero to 3.

PERSONAL ISSUE COMMITMENTS

- CPS: Respondents were determined to be part of an issue public when they said that "issues or problems, ranging from public policy issues to community, family, or personal concerns" led them to get involved in activities. Respondents were also asked whom the issue affected, and if they said that it affected "only other people, but not myself or my family," they were excluded from being in the issue public. Coded as a ratio of the number of instances when respondents said an issue motivated their participation to the number of activities in which they participated. See Chapter 4 for more details.

- ANES: Coded as a dichotomous variable for whether or not the respondent answers "extremely important" to the question, "How important is this issue to YOU?" Survey asks about the following five issues: defense spending, government aid to minorities, abortion, the trade-off between environmental protection and jobs, and the trade-off between government services and spending. See Chapter 3 for more details.

GENERAL INDICATORS OF POLITICIZATION

- Political interest
  - CPS: Constructed as the sum of answers to the following two questions: "Thinking about your local community, how interested are you in local community politics and local community affairs? Are you Very interested, Somewhat interested, Slightly interested, or Not at all interested?" "How interested are you in national politics and national affairs?" 1 = Not interested; 4 = Very interested. Scale ranges from 2 to 8.
  - ANES: Question reads: "Some people don't pay much attention to political campaigns. How about you? Would you say that you were very much interested (3), somewhat interested (2), or not much interested (1) in following the political campaigns this year?" Scale ranges from 1 to 3.
- Political knowledge
  - CPS: Constructed as the sum of dichotomous variables indicating whether the respondent correctly answered eight political information questions. Scale ranges from zero to 8.
  - ANES: Constructed as the sum of dichotomous variables indicating whether the respondent correctly answered four political information questions. Scale ranges from zero to 4.
- Political efficacy
  - CPS: Constructed as the sum of responses to the following questions, asked once about local government and once about national government: "If you had some complaint about a local/national government activity and took that complaint to a member of the local government council, do you think that he or she would pay a lot of attention to what you say, some attention, very little attention, or none at all?" "How much influence do you think someone like you can have over local government decisions—a lot, some, very little, or none at all?" Coded as 1 for none and 4 for a lot. Scale ranges from 4 to 16.
  - ANES: Question reads: "Please tell me how much you agree or disagree with this statement: 'People like me don't have any say about what the government does.'" 1 = Agree strongly; 2 = Agree somewhat; 3 = Neither agree nor disagree; 4 = Disagree somewhat; 5 = Disagree strongly.
- Partisanship
  - CPS: Coded as a 4-point scale constructed from standard party identification questions. Coded as strong partisan (4), weak partisan (3), partisan leaner (2), nonpartisan (1).
  - ANES: Coded as a 4-point scale constructed from standard party identification questions. Coded as strong partisan (4), weak partisan (3), partisan leaner (2), nonpartisan (1).

DEMOGRAPHICS

- Both parents born in the United States
  - CPS: Not included in analysis.
  - ANES: A dichotomous variable for whether or not both of the respondent's parents were born in the United States.

- U.S. citizen
  - CPS: A dichotomous variable for whether or not the respondent is a U.S. citizen.
  - ANES: All respondents in NES studies are citizens of voting age. Not included in analysis.

- English spoken at home
  - CPS: "What language do you usually speak at home—English or something else?" English is scored as 3, English and another language as 2, and another language as 1.
  - ANES: Not included in analysis.

- Working
  - CPS: Coded as 1 = Working full-time; 2 = Working part-time; 3 = Not working.
  - ANES: Dichotomous variable for whether or not the respondent is presently working for pay.

- Retired
  - CPS: Dichotomous variable for whether or not the respondent is presently retired.
  - ANES: Dichotomous variable for whether or not the respondent is presently retired.

- Catholic religious preference
  - CPS: Dichotomous variable for whether or not the respondent is Catholic.
  - ANES: Dichotomous variable for whether or not the respondent is Catholic.

- Age
  - CPS: Dichotomous variables for five age categories: 18–24, 25–34, 35–44, 55–65, and 65 and over (45–54 category is the omitted category)
  - ANES: Included as one variable that is age of the respondent. Ranges from 18 to 93.

Interview Protocol for the
2008 Study of Political Pathways

As discussed in Chapter 5, the protocol below is just a guideline. The questions were not necessarily asked in this order or using the wording below, but all of the interviews covered the topics below. Many interviews also included discussion of other topics not listed in the guidelines below that emerged organically from the discussion. The initial consent form and the demographic questions at the end were read to the interviewees in a standardized way.

INITIAL CONSENT

My name is Hahrie Han, and I am an assistant professor of political science at Wellesley College. I am conducting the Study of Political Pathways, a research study designed to better understand what motivates people to participate in civic and political life. I would like to invite you to participate in this study. If you agree, I will interview you, asking you to describe your involvement in politics and public life, and the kinds of things you think may have been important in getting you involved. The interview will be very open-ended and will take anywhere from thirty minutes to an hour. There are no material benefits or compensation for participating in this study. Through your participation, however, you will be contributing to a better understanding of what motivates people to participate in politics.

Before we begin, I would like to assure you that as a participant in this project, you have certain rights. First, your participation is entirely voluntary. You may refuse to answer any question at any time in the interview, and you may withdraw from the interview at any time. Second, all information collected in this interview will be kept strictly confidential. With your permission, I will record this phone conversation, but only for the purposes of my own notes and record keeping. Excerpts of this interview may be part of the final research report and other written reports, but under no circumstances will your name or any identifying characteristics be included in any written or published materials. In any written or published materials, I will disguise the details of any activities you report, such as the names of organizations, dates, and other information.

First, are you willing to participate in this study?
Second, are you willing to let me tape this interview?

Lastly, before we begin, I'd be happy to share any findings from this study with you. Would you like a copy of the final report? If so, what is the best way to send it to you?

GUIDELINES FOR INTERVIEW QUESTIONS

- Please describe the ways you participate in politics now. Can you describe a typical week or month, in terms of the kind of civic and political work you might do?
- Can you describe the first time you participated in civic or political life? How did you get involved?

- Please describe your journey from that first involvement to your involvement today. Were there any other activities you participated in? Which ones? How did you select them?
- What was your experience like when you first participated? What was your experience like when you first joined the organization?
- When you first got involved or first became a leader, did someone recruit you to participate? Who?
- Was your family very political growing up? Can you describe the ways it was and was not?
- Can you describe an instance when you chose not to get involved? Why?

DEMOGRAPHIC QUESTIONS

Okay, we are almost done. I just have a few standard questions to ask you about your educational background, age, work experience, income, and other such things. I know some of these questions might feel very personal, or even redundant because they already came up in our discussion. I'm asking these questions because I want to be able to compare the group of people that I interview to national samples of participants to see how they compare in important demographic categories. I would appreciate it if you were willing to answer them.

- In what year were you born?
- Last week, were you working full-time for pay, working part-time for pay, retired, going to school, or something else?
- If working, what kind of work do you normally do?
- What is the highest grade of regular school that you have completed and gotten credit for? (By regular school we mean a school that can be counted toward an elementary or high school diploma or a college or university degree.)
  - Did you get a high school diploma or pass a high school equivalency test?
  - Do you have any college degrees—that is, not including degrees from a business college, technical college, or vocational school?
  - What is the highest degree that you have earned?
- How would you describe your racial background?
- Are you an American citizen?
- Were your parents born abroad or in the United States?
- Were you born in the United States?
- I am going to read a list of income categories to you. Please tell me which of the income groups best describes the total 2007 income before taxes of all members of your family living in your home? Please include salaries, wages, pensions, dividends, interest, and all other income. If uncertain, what would be your best guess?
  - Under $5,000
  - $5,000–$9,999
  - $10,000–$14,999
  - $15,000–$19,999
  - $20,000–$24,999
  - $25,000–$29,999
  - $30,000–$34,999
  - $35,000–$39,999
  - $40,000–$49,999

- $50,000–$59,999
- $60,000–$74,999
- $75,000–$99,999
- $100,000–$124,999
- $125,000–$149,999
- $150,000–$199,999
- $200,000 and over

The 2003 National Purpose, Local Action Study

The National Purpose, Local Action project was conducted in the summer of 2003 as a result of discussions with Sierra Club leaders concerned about the unrealized potential of their 750,000 members, 343 local groups, and 62 chapters. In the complete study, there were five different data sources. In this book, only data from the ExCom Leader Survey (ELS) was used. These are written surveys with Sierra Club Executive Committee (ExCom) members on background, leadership, and organizational practices. The fifteen-page ELS was completed by 1,624 ExCom members. The surveys were completed prior to participation in local meetings to assess organizational practices led by volunteer facilitators and conducted from October 2003 to February 2004. The survey includes closed-ended and open-ended questions on the background, leadership experience, goals and motivations, and organizational practices of local leaders, as well as their evaluation of the practices and efficacy of their own ExCom. A description of the variables from this study that were included in the analysis in this book follows.

Now, take some time to think about the long-term goals, values, and motivations that led you to become active in the Sierra Club. What were your long-term goals? Check the box next to your top THREE goals. Then, circle the *ONE* long-term goal that is most important to you.

- Enjoy/explore the outdoors
- Influence politics and public policy to protect the environment
- Protect natural environments
- Meet/work with like-minded people
- Influence public opinion
- Become a more effective advocate/activist/leader
- Fulfill moral/civic responsibilities
- Strengthen the Sierra Club

Please take a moment to think about how you feel about your experience as a volunteer leader in the Sierra Club. Circle the appropriate response to indicate how much you agree with each statement ranging from "Strongly Disagree" (1) to "Strongly Agree" (5).

- My work in the Sierra Club influences many aspects of my life.
- I really feel as if the ExCom's problems are my problems.
- I often try to think of ways of doing my work on the ExCom more effectively.
- I feel myself to be part of the ExCom in which I work.
- What the Sierra Club stands for is very important to me.
- I am proud to tell others that I am part of the Sierra Club.

Notes

CHAPTER I

1. Data from the Louisiana Elections Division.
2. For a summary, see Schlozman, "Citizen Participation in America."
3. Quotation and statistics from Konigsmark, "New Orleans' Upheaval."
4. Komp, "Despite Barriers."
5. "Nagin Re-elected."
6. Quoted in Moreno, "Displaced Voters Make Wishes Known."
7. Bartels, *Unequal Democracy.*
8. Scholars have a long history of looking empirically and theoretically at multiple models of representation. See, for example, Fairlie, "Nature of Political Representation, I"; Fairlie, "Nature of Political Representation, II"; Dahl, *Preface to Democratic Theory*; Pitkin, *Concept of Representation*; Fiorina, *Representatives, Roll Calls, and Constituencies*; Weissberg, "Collective Versus Dyadic Representation"; Mansbridge, "Rethinking Representation"; Stimson, MacKuen, and Erikson, "Dynamic Representation"; Bartels, "Constituency Opinion"; and Warren Miller and Stokes, "Constituency Influence in Congress." However, systematic studies of representation that identify which groups of people have more influence than others have just begun to emerge. Most studies aggregate individuals across congressional districts, states, or the nation. Much theoretical literature, however, has argued that legislators do differentiate their constituents based on how likely they are to vote and help the legislator get reelected. See, for instance, Fenno, *Home Style*; and Kingdon, *Congressmen's Voting Decisions.*
9. Studies about the effect of wealth on representation include Bartels, "Inequality and Popular Sovereignty"; and Gilens, "Public Opinion and Democratic Responsiveness." Studies about the effect of partisanship on representation include Holian, Krebs, and Walsh, "Constituency Opinion"; Wright, "Policy Voting in the U.S. Senate"; and Shapiro et al., "Linking Constituency Opinion and Senate Voting Scores."
10. Task Force on Inequality and American Democracy, *American Democracy*, 2.
11. Lohmann, "Signaling Model."
12. Ainsworth and Sened, "Role of Lobbyists"; Austin-Smith, "Information and Influence"; Austin-Smith, "Campaign Contributions and Access."
13. Schlozman, "Citizen Participation in America"; Brady, "Political Participation."
14. Schlozman, "Citizen Participation in America."
15. See, for example, Verba, Schlozman, and Brady, *Voice and Equality*; Rosenstone and Hansen, *Mobilization, Participation, and Democracy in America*; Wolfinger and Rosenstone, *Who Votes?*; and Verba and Nie, *Participation in America.*
16. See, for example, Schlozman, "Citizen Participation in America"; Verba, Schlozman, and Brady, *Voice and Equality*; and Rosenstone and Hansen, *Mobilization, Participation, and Democracy in America.*

17. Aldrich, "Positive Theory and Voice and Equality"; Fiorina, "Parties, Participation, and Representation in America"; Brady, "Political Participation."

18. In "Parties, Participation, and Representation in America," Fiorina cites the resource-mobilization model in Verba, Schlozman, and Brady, *Voice and Equality*, as the dominant model of participation.

19. See, for instance, Verba, Schlozman, and Brady, *Voice and Equality*; Verba and Nie, *Participation in America*; and Wolfinger and Rosenstone, *Who Votes?*

20. See, for instance, Rosenstone and Hansen, *Mobilization, Participation, and Democracy in America*; and Robert Huckfeldt and John Sprague, *Citizens, Politics and Social Communication*.

21. Rosenstone and Hansen, *Mobilization, Participation, and Democracy in America*; Gerber and Green, "Effects of Canvassing."

22. Fiorina, "Parties, Participation, and Representation in America"; Aldrich, "Positive Theory and Voice and Equality"; Brady, "Political Participation."

23. Wolfinger and Rosenstone, *Who Votes?*; Rosenstone and Hansen, *Mobilization, Participation, and Democracy in America*; Verba, Schlozman, and Brady, *Voice and Equality*; Plutzer, "Becoming a Habitual Voter"; Verba and Nie, *Participation in America*; Robinson, Shaver, and Wrightsman, *Measures of Political Attitudes*.

24. Schlozman, "Citizen Participation in America," 439.

25. Brady, "Political Participation," 796.

26. Aldrich, "Positive Theory and Voice and Equality," 423.

27. Fiorina, "Parties, Participation, and Representation in America."

28. Both of these people were interviewed for the Study of Political Pathways, described in greater detail in Chapter 5. In all quotations from the study used throughout the book, names have been changed to protect the confidentiality of the subjects.

29. Converse, "Nature of Belief Systems."

30. See, for example, Schlozman and Verba, *Injury to Insult*; and Rosenstone and Hansen, *Mobilization, Participation, and Democracy in America*.

31. Brader, *Campaigning for Hearts and Minds*; Marcus, Neuman, and MacKuen, *Affective Intelligence and Political Judgment*.

32. Weiner, "History of Motivational Research in Education"; Martin Ford, *Motivating Humans*; Pittman, "Motivation."

33. Nussbaum, *Upheavals of Thought*; Zajonc, "Emotions"; Marcus, *Sentimental Citizen*; Damasio, *Descartes' Error*; Gray, "Neuropsychology of Emotion and Personality"; Richard Lane and Nadel, *Cognitive Neuroscience of Emotion*.

34. There is currently a debate about whether emotions and cognition work together or whether one precedes the other in motivating action. Although I am primarily interested in the role of emotions in energizing behavior, that focus does not preclude the role of cognition. Ford, *Motivating Humans*; Pittman, "Motivation."

35. Brader, *Campaigning for Hearts and Minds*; Marcus, Neuman, and MacKuen, *Affective Intelligence and Political Judgment*.

36. See, for example, Verba, Schlozman, and Brady, *Voice and Equality*; Rosenstone and Hansen, *Mobilization, Participation, and Democracy in America*.

37. See, for example, Sapiro, "Not Your Parents' Political Socialization"; Youniss and Yates, *Community Service and Social Responsibility in Youth*; Stoker and Jennings, "Life-Cycle Transitions and Political Participation"; Jennings, "American Political Participation"; Jennings and Niemi, *Political Character in Adolescence*.

38. Andrea Campbell, *How Policies Make Citizens.*
39. See Krosnick and Telhami, "Public Attitudes Toward Israel" for an example.
40. Schier, *By Invitation Only.*
41. Taddeo, "Man Who Made Obama."
42. Netroots Nation Conference, July 19, 2008, Austin, TX.
43. Andrea Campbell, *How Policies Make Citizens*; Skocpol, *Protecting Soldiers and Mothers*; Pierson, "When Effect Becomes Cause."
44. See, for instance, Verba, Schlozman, and Brady, *Voice and Equality*; and Rosenstone and Hansen, *Mobilization, Participation, and Democracy in America.*
45. Schier, *By Invitation Only.*

CHAPTER 2

1. See Verba, Schlozman, and Brady, *Voice and Equality*, for a classic expression of this model.
2. Leighley, *Strength in Numbers?*; Schier, *By Invitation Only.*
3. For contextual effects on participation, see, for example, Leighley, *Strength in Numbers?*; Zuckerman, *Social Logic of Politics*; and Mutz, *Impersonal Influence.* For the role of emotion, see Marcus, *Sentimental Citizen*; and Brader, *Campaigning for Hearts and Minds.*
4. Joanne Miller, "Why Do Individuals Participate in Politics?"; Schuessler, *Logic of Expressive Choice.*
5. Dahl, *Who Governs?* 305.
6. Berelson, Lazarsfeld, and McPhee, *Voting* (1966); Angus Campbell et al., *American Voter*; Converse, "Nature of Belief Systems"; Zaller, *Nature and Origin of Mass Opinion.*
7. See, for example, Converse, "Nature of Belief Systems"; Hutchings, *Public Opinion and Democratic Accountability*; Krosnick, "Government Policy and Citizen Passion."
8. Fiorina, "Parties, Participation, and Representation in America"; Brady, "Political Participation"; Aldrich, "Positive Theory and Voice and Equality."
9. Rosenstone and Hansen, *Mobilization, Participation, and Democracy in America*, 20.
10. Schlozman, "Citizen Participation in America," 439.
11. Verba, Schlozman, and Brady, *Voice and Equality*; Rosenstone and Hansen, *Mobilization, Participation, and Democracy in America*; Wolfinger and Rosenstone, *Who Votes?*; Verba and Nie, *Participation in America*; Schlozman, "Citizen Participation in America."
12. Schier, *By Invitation Only*; Hans Nichols, "Hill Dems Get into Demzilla"; Kari Lundgren, "Welcome to the Age of Consumer Politics"; Edsall and Grimaldi, "GOP Got More Bang for Its Billion"; Bai, "Multilevel Marketing of the President."
13. Edsall and Grimaldi, "GOP Got More Bang for Its Billion."
14. Wilson, *Political Organizations*; Joanne Miller and Rahn, "Identity-Based Feelings, Beliefs, and Actions"; Joanne Miller, "Why Do Individuals Participate in Politics?"; Schlozman, Verba, and Brady, "Participation's Not a Paradox."
15. Wilson, *Political Organizations.*
16. Schlozman, Verba, and Brady, "Participation's Not a Paradox."
17. Joanne Miller, "Why Do Individuals Participate in Politics?"
18. Downs, *Economic Theory of Democracy*; Olson, *Logic of Collective Action.*

19. Fiorina, "Information and Rationality in Elections."

20. This applies to most classic studies of participation, including but not limited to Rosenstone and Hansen, *Mobilization, Participation, and Democracy in America*; Verba, Schlozman, and Brady, *Voice and Equality*; Leighley, *Strength in Numbers?*

21. Riker and Ordeshook, "Theory of the Calculus of Voting"; Fiorina, "Voting Decision"; Overbye, "Making a Case"; Schuessler, *Logic of Expressive Choice*.

22. Calvert, "Identity, Expression, and Rational Choice Theory."

23. Fiorina, "Parties, Participation, and Representation in America."

24. Rosenstone and Hansen, *Mobilization, Participation, and Democracy in America*, 16.

25. Wilson, *Political Organizations*; Schlozman, Verba, and Brady, "Participation's Not a Paradox."

26. See, for example, Miller, "Why Do Individuals Participate in Politics?"; Wilson, *Political Organizations*.

27. For a summary, see Calvert, "Identity, Expression, and Rational Choice Theory."

28. Pittman, "Motivation"; Martin Ford, *Motivating Humans*.

29. I thank Paul Sniderman for key insights on this point.

30. Wolfinger, "Rational Citizen," 84.

31. Quoted in Cassidy, "Mind Games," 34.

32. Schlozman and Verba, *Injury to Insult*. They do acknowledge the likelihood of a feedback loop between the fifth step and some of the prior steps. They do not, however, explore this in great depth in their work.

33. Weiner, "History of Motivational Research in Education"; Martin Ford, *Motivating Humans*. This emotional processing occurs not only when we are conscious of it—when we meet someone new for the first time, for instance—but also when we are wholly unaware of it. Multiple studies have found that many human behaviors are governed by habitual reactions to external stimuli. Bargh and Chartrand, "Unbearable Automaticity of Being"; Damasio, *Descartes' Error*; Schacter, *Searching for Memory*; Willingham, "Neuropsychological Theory."

34. *Merriam-Webster Online*, http://www.m-w.com.

35. Pittman, "Motivation," 549.

36. Some scholars argue that characteristics like personal efficacy and perceptions of control are also fundamental to motivation (Bandura, *Self-Efficacy*; D. H. Ford and Lerner, *Developmental Systems Theory*). People are more likely to take action if they think the action will be successful. D. H. Ford, however, points out that this evaluation of how "successful" an action is likely to be occurs in the context of emotions and personal goals. Without a desired end state, the individual lacks a metric to evaluate "success." Because emotions and personal goals appear to be prior to the other factors, I focus on these elements. This should not, however, minimize the importance of these other factors in motivation. See Pittman, "Motivation," for a review of some of these other factors.

37. Note that this does not mean that emotion is solely responsible for action, independent of cognition.

38. Nussbaum, *Upheavals of Thought*; Zajonc, "Emotions"; Marcus, *Sentimental Citizen*; Damasio, *Descartes' Error*.

39. Damasio, *Descartes' Error*; Marcus, *Sentimental Citizen*; Gray, "Neuropsychology of Emotion and Personality"; Richard Lane and Nadel, *Cognitive Neuroscience of Emotion*.

40. At any moment, emotional systems serve several critical functions in directing our behavior (Damasio, *Descartes' Error*; Marcus, *Sentimental Citizen*; Gray, "Neuropsychology of Emotion and Personality"; Richard Lane and Nadel, *Cognitive Neuroscience of Emotion*). First, they monitor the copious, ongoing sensations that we receive from the people and world around us. My emotional systems interpret the sensation of heat on my fingers to tell me the pot is too hot to touch. Likewise, they interpret the look of amusement on someone's face to tell me if I am being funny. Depending on whether I am trying to be funny or not, my emotions react to the look of amusement positively or negatively. Second, emotions provide real-time feedback about a current situation to help adjust behavior. If I was trying to be funny and the other person did not laugh, my emotion systems would return a negative feeling. This negative emotion might stop me from telling another joke. Third, emotions use past experience to evaluate plans for future action relative to current stimuli. This helps us decide whether our plans will have the desired effect. If someone is not laughing when I am trying to be funny, how should I respond? My emotion systems use past experiences to develop an appropriate response. Marcus, *Sentimental Citizen*, provides an excellent summary of how these neurological systems work. The two emotion systems that provide these functions and are important to political behavior are the behavioral activation, or "disposition" system, and the behavioral inhibition, or "surveillance" system. Both systems act as monitors of incoming information about the world. The behavioral activation system uses information from past experiences to determine if an action was successful or unsuccessful. If successful, then the system returns positive feelings such as happiness or enthusiasm. If an action was unsuccessful or questionable, the behavioral activation system returns negative feelings. The behavioral inhibition system helps with new situations. When new sensations can be processed using past experiences, the behavioral inhibition system returns feelings of calmness. When the new sensations do not meet expectations based on past experiences, the behavioral inhibition system returns feelings of anxiety or nervousness that may prompt conscious processing or action.

41. Pittman, "Motivation," 550.

42. See, for example, Berelson, Lazarsfeld, and McPhee, *Voting*; Angus Campbell et al., *American Voter*; Robert Lane, *Political Ideology*.

43. Angus Campbell et al., *American Voter*, 76.

44. Rosenstone and Hansen, *Mobilization, Participation, and Democracy in America*.

45. See, for example, Leighley, *Strength in Numbers?*; Tate, *From Protest to Politics*; Harris, *Something Within*.

46. Gerber, Green, and Larimer, "Social Pressure and Voter Turnout"; Nickerson, "Is Voting Contagious?"

47. Leighley, *Strength in Numbers?*; Harris, *Something Within*; Tate, *From Protest to Politics*.

48. Nussbaum, *Upheavals of Thought*.

49. Rosenstone and Hansen, *Mobilization, Participation, and Democracy in America*, 20.

50. Schlozman and Verba, *Injury to Insult*, 332.

51. See, for instance, Fisher, *Activism, Inc.*

52. Nussbaum, *Upheavals of Thought*, 31.

53. Frijda, "Laws of Emotion"; Pervin, "Self-Regulation"; Lazarus, "Cognitive-Motivational-Relational Theory of Emotion"; Martin Ford, *Motivating Humans*.

54. Nussbaum, *Upheavals of Thought*, 31–32.

55. Teske, *Political Activists in America*, 96.

56. Nussbaum, *Upheavals of Thought*, 31.

57. Brader, *Campaigning for Hearts and Minds*.

58. See, for instance, Valentino, Hutchings, and White, "Cues That Matter."

59. Chong and Druckman, "Framing Theory."

60. Smith, *Stories of Peoplehood*.

CHAPTER 3

1. *Public Knowledge of Current Affairs.*

2. Converse, "Nature of Belief Systems," 245.

3. Krosnick, "Role of Attitude Importance"; Krosnick, "Government Policy and Citizen Passion."

4. Hutchings, *Public Opinion and Democratic Accountability*.

5. See Boninger, Krosnick, and Berent, "Origins of Attitude Importance," on the relationship between extremity and issue publics.

6. See, for example, Aldrich, Sullivan, and Borgida, "Foreign Affairs and Issue Voting"; Niemi and Bartels, "New Measures of Issue Salience"; Kessel, "Issues in Issue Voting"; and RePass, "Issue Salience and Party Choice."

7. Laitin, *Identity in Formation*.

8. Gutmann, "Identity and Democracy."

9. Berelson, Lazarsfeld, and McPhee, *Voting*; Angus Campbell et al., *American Voter*.

10. Converse, "Nature of Belief Systems."

11. Zaller, *Nature and Origin of Mass Opinion*.

12. Converse, "Nature of Belief Systems."

13. Almond, *American People and Foreign Policy*.

14. Carpini and Keeter, *What Americans Know About Politics*; Zaller, *Nature and Origin of Mass Opinion*.

15. Gershkoff, "Not 'Non-Attitudes'"; Hutchings, *Public Opinion and Democratic Accountability*; Krosnick, "Government Policy and Citizen Passion"; Krosnick, "Role of Attitude Importance."

16. Gilens, "Public Opinion and Democratic Responsiveness."

17. Price and Zaller, "Who Gets the News?"

18. Converse, "Nature of Belief Systems"; Krosnick, "Government Policy and Citizen Passion"; Krosnick, "Role of Attitude Importance."

19. Krosnick, "Government Policy and Citizen Passion," 72.

20. Robert Lane, *Political Ideology*.

21. Downs, *Economic Theory of Democracy*; Kuklinski and Quirk, "Reconsidering the Rational Public."

22. See, for example, Page and Shapiro, "Effects of Public Opinion on Policy"; Verba, Schlozman, and Brady, *Voice and Equality*.

23. Boninger, Krosnick, and Berent, "Origins of Attitude Importance," 171–72.

24. See, for example, Wolfinger and Rosenstone, *Who Votes?*

25. Gershkoff, "Not 'Non-Attitudes.'"

26. Gershkoff, "Not 'Non-Attitudes,'" tests this by looking at the number of people with policy commitments using closed-ended self-report questions and the number of people

using open-ended questions. She finds that open-ended questions result in fewer people with strong commitments. In using the closed-ended questions, however, she defines political commitment by the proportion of respondents who say that an issue is "very important" or "extremely important" to them, the top two items on the five-point response scale. If, however, she were to define issue publics as only the people who say an issue is "extremely important" to them (as they are defined in this book), then the proportions of people with political commitment in the population are comparable to her findings using open-ended questions.

27. Kessel, "Issues in Issue Voting," 461.

28. Krosnick, "Government Policy and Citizen Passion"; Krosnick, "Role of Attitude Importance"; Krosnick and Telhami, "Public Attitudes Toward Israel."

29. Krosnick, "Government Policy and Citizen Passion"; Krosnick, "Role of Attitude Importance."

30. See Appendix A for the specific survey questions used in each year and details on coding of the variables used in this chapter.

31. Krosnick, "Government Policy and Citizen Passion"; Krosnick, "Role of Attitude Importance"; Krosnick and Telhami, "Public Attitudes Toward Israel."

32. Fiorina, "Parties, Participation, and Representation in America."

33. Schlozman, Verba, and Brady, "Participation's Not a Paradox."

34. Nussbaum, *Upheavals of Thought*; Marcus, *Sentimental Citizen*.

35. See Appendix A for details on how personal commitments were measured in each year of the American National Election Study.

36. Boninger, Krosnick, and Berent, "Origins of Attitude Importance"; Schuman and Presser, *Questions and Answers*.

37. Higgins and King, "Accessibility of Social Constructs."

38. Krosnick, "Government Policy and Citizen Passion"; Krosnick, "Role of Attitude Importance"; Gershkoff, "Not 'Non-Attitudes'"; Hutchings, *Public Opinion and Democratic Accountability*.

39. Krosnick, "Government Policy and Citizen Passion"; Krosnick, "Role of Attitude Importance."

40. Krosnick, "Government Policy and Citizen Passion"; Krosnick, "Role of Attitude Importance"; Gershkoff, "Not 'Non-Attitudes'"; Hutchings, *Public Opinion and Democratic Accountability*.

41. Schlozman, "Citizen Participation in America."

42. "High" and "low" political interest is assessed by dividing respondents into terciles based on their expressed level of political interest. "High" political interest respondents are those in the top tercile; "low" political interest respondents are those in the bottom tercile.

CHAPTER 4

1. Branch, *Parting the Waters*, 145–46.

2. See, for instance, Verba, Schlozman, and Brady, *Voice and Equality*; Rosenstone and Hansen, *Mobilization, Participation, and Democracy in America*; Wolfinger and Rosenstone, *Who Votes?*; and Verba and Nie, *Participation in America*.

3. Wolfinger and Rosenstone, *Who Votes?*; Angus Campbell et al., *American Voter*; Verba, Schlozman, and Brady, *Voice and Equality*.

4. See the discussion of measuring issue publics in Chapter 3.

5. Jennings and Andersen, "Importance of Social and Political Context."

6. Visser, Krosnick, and Simmons, "Cognitive and Behavioral Consequences."

7. Schlozman, Verba, and Brady, "Participation's Not a Paradox."

8. Jennings and Andersen, "Importance of Social and Political Context."

9. Visser, Krosnick, and Simmons, "Cognitive and Behavioral Consequences"; Joanne Miller et al., "Impact of Policy Change Threat."

10. Verba, Schlozman, and Brady, *Voice and Equality*; Fiorina, "Parties, Participation, and Representation in America."

11. See Verba, Schlozman, and Brady, *Voice and Equality*, Appendix D.

12. See, for example, ibid.; Rosenstone and Hansen, *Mobilization, Participation, and Democracy in America*; Wolfinger and Rosenstone, *Who Votes?*; Verba and Nie, *Participation in America*.

13. Verba, Schlozman, and Brady, *Voice and Equality*.

14. Nie, Junn, and Stehlik-Barry, *Education and Democratic Citizenship in America*.

15. Verba, Schlozman, and Brady, *Voice and Equality*, chap. 11.

16. Schlozman and Verba, *Injury to Insult*, 332.

17. Nie, Junn, and Stehlik-Barry, *Education and Democratic Citizenship in America*.

18. Mayhew, *Congress*.

19. See, for example, Binder and Smith, *Politics or Principle?*; Schickler, *Disjointed Pluralism*; Canes-Wrone, Brady, and Cogan, "Out of Step, Out of Office"; Jones, "Speculative Augmentation."

20. Johnson, Wahlbeck, and Spriggs, "Influence of Oral Arguments."

21. Citrin and Green, "Self-Interest Motive."

22. Fiorina, "Comment"; Wolfinger, "Rational Citizen."

CHAPTER 5

1. Teske, *Political Activists in America*.

2. "Terence" is the pseudonym Teske uses to protect the confidentiality of the individual.

3. Teske, *Political Activists in America*, 1–2.

4. Ibid.

5. Petty and Krosnick, *Attitude Strength*; Boninger, Krosnick, and Berent, "Origins of Attitude Importance."

6. Hansen, *Gaining Access*.

7. Teske, *Political Activists in America*.

8. See also Chapter 3 for a discussion of how Hutchings's definition of issue publics differs from the one used throughout this book. Despite these differences, his insights on the role of context in shaping issue public membership are relevant.

9. Hutchings, *Public Opinion and Democratic Accountability*, 4.

10. Sapiro, "Not Your Parents' Political Socialization," 3.

11. See, for example, ibid.; Jennings and Niemi, *Generations and Politics*; Plutzer, "Becoming a Habitual Voter"; Green and Shachar, "Habit-Formation and Political Behavior."

12. Galston, "Political Knowledge"; McClellan and Youniss, "Two Systems of Youth Service"; Kirlin, "Adult Civic Engagement"; Youniss, McLellan, and Yates, "Engendering Civic Identity." This is also consistent with research on the effect of political context on

political participation, particularly minority participation (Leighley, *Strength in Numbers?*; Harris, *Something Within*). These scholars find that people's communities can play an important role in developing the motivational resources they need to participate.

13. McAdam, *Freedom Summer.*

14. Youniss, McLellan, and Yates, "Engendering Civic Identity."

15. Haste and Torney-Purta, introduction to *Development of Political Understanding.*

16. Teske, *Political Activists in America*, 21.

17. Miller and Rahn, "Identity-Based Feelings, Beliefs, and Actions."

18. Almond and Verba, *Civic Culture*; Hyman, *Political Socialization*; Sapiro, "Not Your Parents' Political Socialization"; Jennings and Niemi, *Generations and Politics*; Jennings and Niemi, *Political Character in Adolescence*; Galston, "Political Knowledge"; McClellan and Youniss, "Two Systems of Youth Service."

19. Bargh and Chartrand, "Unbearable Automaticity of Being"; Chartrand and Bargh, "Chameleon Effect"; Zuckerman, *Social Logic of Politics.*

20. Damasio, *Descartes' Error*; LeDoux, "Emotional Memory Systems"; Marcus, *Sentimental Citizen.*

21. Bargh and Chartrand, "Unbearable Automaticity of Being"; Damasio, *Descartes' Error*; Schacter, *Searching for Memory*; Willingham, "Neuropsychological Theory."

22. Ganz et al., "Against the Tide," 152.

23. McAdam, *Freedom Summer*; McAdam, "Biographical Consequences of Activism"; Teske, "Beyond Altruism."

24. Similar sampling methods have been used in other studies, such as Strolovitch, *Affirmative Advocacy*, and Baumgartner, *Conflict and Rhetoric.*

25. See table A-2 ("Percent of People 25 Years and Over Who Have Completed High School or College, by Race, Hispanic Origin and Sex: Selected Years 1940 to 2007") of the Current Population Survey, http://www.census.gov/population/www/socdemo/educ-attn.html.

26. Schlozman, Verba, and Brady, "Participation's Not a Paradox," 2.

27. Nisbett and Wilson, "Telling More Than We Can Know."

28. Teske, *Political Activists in America.*

29. For a summary, see Sapiro, "Not Your Parents' Political Socialization."

30. Rosenstone and Hansen, *Mobilization, Participation, and Democracy in America*; Gerber and Green, "Effects of Canvassing."

31. Walker, *Mobilizing Interest Groups in America*; Wilson, *Political Organizations*; Schlozman, Verba, and Brady, "Participation's Not a Paradox."

32. Walker, *Mobilizing Interest Groups in America.*

33. See Appendix D for more information on the National Purpose, Local Action Study and the specific survey questions used in analysis.

34. Berry, *New Liberalism*; Meyer and Tarrow, *Social Movement Society*; Putnam, *Bowling Alone.*

35. Amenta, Caren, and Olasky, "Just the Facts."

36. Skocpol, *Diminished Democracy*; Skocpol, Ganz, and Munson, "Nation of Organizers."

37. Ganz, "Resources and Resourcefulness"; Andrews et al., "Explaining Effectiveness."

38. Verba, Schlozman, and Brady, *Voice and Equality.*

CHAPTER 6

1. Waldman, "Myth of the Rational Iowa Voter."
2. The turnout percentage comes from Michael McDonald's United States Elections Project, at http://elections.gmu.edu/Turnout_2008P.html.
3. Bartels, "Inequality and Popular Sovereignty"; Hacker and Pierson, "Abandoning the Middle"; Gilens, "Public Opinion and Democratic Responsiveness."
4. Hans Nichols, "Hill Dems Get into Demzilla"; Lundgren, "Welcome to the Age of Consumer Politics."
5. Schier, *By Invitation Only.*
6. Hillygus and Shields, *Persuadable Voter.*
7. Quoted in Weigel, "Political Bull's-Eye."
8. Quoted in Lundgren, "Welcome to the Age of Consumer Politics."
9. Naturally, it is quite possible that being recruited to participate by a political party increases an individual's level of interest. To mitigate this problem, I drew on the measure of political interest in the ANES presurvey, prior to the bulk of the campaign season when respondents were likely to have been contacted. In this and subsequent graphs, "high" levels of political interest are defined as those in the top third of the distribution, while "low" levels of interest are defined as those in the bottom third.
10. Skocpol, *Diminished Democracy*; Skocpol, Ganz, and Munson, "Nation of Organizers"; Schier, *By Invitation Only*; Key, *Politics, Parties, and Pressure Groups.*
11. Skocpol, *Diminished Democracy*; Skocpol, Ganz, and Munson, "Nation of Organizers."
12. Skocpol, *Diminished Democracy.*
13. Kornbluh, *Why America Stopped Voting.*
14. Ibid., 19.
15. Ostrogorski, *Democracy*, 333.
16. Kornbluh, *Why America Stopped Voting*, 41.
17. McGerr, *Decline of Popular Politics.*
18. Ostrogorski, *Democracy*, 290–91.
19. Wiebe, *Search for Order*; Gould, "Party Conflict."
20. Wiebe, *Search for Order*, 30–32.
21. Schlesinger, "Primary Goals of Political Parties"; Schlesinger, *Political Parties.*
22. Salisbury, "Urban Party Organization Member"; Aldrich, *Why Parties?*; Wilson, *Amateur Democrat*; Polsby and Wildavsky, *Presidential Elections*; Key, *Politics, Parties, and Pressure Groups.*
23. Goodwyn, *Populist Movement.*
24. Ibid., 19.
25. Walker, "Interests, Political Parties, and Policy Formation."
26. Ibid., 69.
27. Schier, *By Invitation Only.*
28. Goodwyn, *Populist Movement*, xxi.
29. Golis, "War for Field Organizing"; Exley, "Stories and Numbers"; Martelle, "Political Machine."
30. Raum and Pickler, "Obama Seals Nomination"; Shepard, "Elements of Obama's Successful Campaign."
31. Martelle, "Famed Organizer."
32. Quoted in Garofoli, "Obama Backers Get Neighborly."

33. Bernstein, "State Dems Banking on Youth, Diversity"; Bender, "'Aloha Spirit' Lifts Obama."

34. Skocpol, *Diminished Democracy*; Schier, *By Invitation Only*; Kornbluh, *Why America Stopped Voting*.

35. See, for example, Task Force on Inequality and American Democracy, *American Democracy*.

36. See, for example, Verba, Schlozman, and Brady, *Voice and Equality*; Rosenstone and Hansen, *Mobilization, Participation, and Democracy in America*; Wolfinger and Rosenstone, *Who Votes?*; Verba and Nie, *Participation in America*.

37. Bill Nichols, "More Voters Aren't Waiting."

38. Woodwell, *Thinking Outside the Ballot Box*, 1.

Bibliography

Ainsworth, Scott, and Itai Sened. "The Role of Lobbyists: Entrepreneurs with Two Audiences." *American Journal of Political Science* 37, no. 3 (1993): 834–66.

Aldrich, John. "Positive Theory and Voice and Equality." *American Political Science Review* 91, no. 2 (1997): 421–23.

———. *Why Parties?* Chicago: University of Chicago Press, 1995.

Aldrich, John H., John L. Sullivan, and Eugene Borgida. "Foreign Affairs and Issue Voting: Do Presidential Candidates 'Waltz Before a Blind Audience'?" *American Political Science Review* 83, no. 1 (1989): 123–41.

Almond, Gabriel. *The American People and Foreign Policy*. New York: Praeger, 1950.

Almond, Gabriel, and Sidney Verba. *The Civic Culture*. Princeton, NJ: Princeton University Press, 1963.

Amenta, Edwin, Neal Caren, and Sheera Olasky. "Just the Facts: Newspaper Coverage of Social Movement Organizations in the 20th Century." *Contexts* 4, no. 3 (2005): 48–49.

Andrews, Kenneth T., Marshall Ganz, Matthew Baggetta, Hahrie Han, and Chaeyoon Lim. "Leadership, Membership, and Voice: Civic Associations That Work." Forthcoming in *American Journal of Sociology*.

Austin-Smith, David. "Campaign Contributions and Access." *American Political Science Review* 89, no. 3 (1995): 566–81.

———. "Information and Influence: Lobbying for Agendas and Votes." *American Journal of Political Science* 37 (1993): 799–833.

Bai, Matt. "The Multilevel Marketing of the President." *New York Times Magazine*, April 25, 2004.

Bandura, Albert. *Self-Efficacy: The Exercise of Control*. New York: W. H. Freeman and Co., 1997.

Bargh, John A., and Tanya L. Chartrand. "The Unbearable Automaticity of Being." *American Psychologist* 54, no. 7 (1999): 462–79.

Bartels, Larry M. "Constituency Opinion and Congressional Policy Making: The Reagan Defense Build Up." *American Political Science Review* 85, no. 2 (1991): 457–74.

———. *Unequal Democracy: The Political Economy of a New Gilded Age*. Princeton, NJ: Princeton University Press, 2008.

Baumgartner, Frank. *Conflict and Rhetoric in French Policymaking*. Pittsburgh: University of Pittsburgh Press, 1989.

Bender, Bryan. "'Aloha Spirit' Lifts Obama: Native Son's Vision of Inclusiveness Echoes Hawaii's Multicultural Heritage." *Boston Globe*, February 21, 2008.

Berelson, Bernard R., Paul F. Lazarsfeld, and William N. McPhee. *Voting: A Study of Opinion Formation in a Presidential Campaign*. Chicago: University of Chicago Press, 1954; reprint University of Chicago Press Phoenix Books, 1966.

Bernstein, Alan. "State Dems Banking on Youth, Diversity: Thousands of First-Time Delegates to Fill Convention This Week in Austin." *Houston Chronicle*, June 1, 2008.

Berry, Jeffrey M. *The New Liberalism: The Rising Power of Citizen Groups*. Washington, DC: Brookings Institution Press, 1999.

Binder, Sarah, and Steven Smith. *Politics or Principle? Filibustering in the United States Senate*. Washington, DC: Brookings Institution, 1997.

Boninger, David S., Jon A. Krosnick, and Matthew K. Berent. "Origins of Attitude Importance: Self-Interest, Social Identification, and Value Relevance." *Journal of Personality and Social Psychology* 68, no. 1 (1995): 61–80.

Brader, Ted. *Campaigning for Hearts and Minds: How Emotional Appeals in Political Ads Work*. Chicago: University of Chicago Press, 2006.

Brady, Henry E. "Political Participation." In Robinson, Shaver, and Wrightsman, *Measures of Political Attitudes*, 737–800.

Branch, Taylor. *Parting the Waters: America in the King Years 1954–63*. New York: Simon and Schuster, 1989.

Calvert, Randall. "Identity, Expression, and Rational Choice Theory." In *Political Science: State of the Discipline*, edited by Ira Katznelson and Helen Milner, 568–96. New York: American Political Science Association / W. W. Norton, 2002.

Campbell, Andrea. *How Policies Make Citizens: Senior Citizen Activism and the American Welfare State*. Princeton, NJ: Princeton University Press, 2003.

Campbell, Angus, Philip E. Converse, Warren E. Miller, and Donald E. Stokes. *The American Voter*. New York: Wiley, 1960.

Canes-Wrone, Brandice, David W. Brady, and John F. Cogan. "Out of Step, Out of Office: Electoral Accountability and House Members' Voting." *American Political Science Review* 96, no. 1 (2002): 127–40.

Cassidy, John. "Mind Games: What Neuroeconomics Tells Us About Money and the Brain." *New Yorker*, September 18, 2006, 30–37.

Chartrand, Tanya L., and John A. Bargh. "The Chameleon Effect: The Perception-Behavior Link and Social Interaction." *Journal of Personality and Social Psychology* 76 (1999): 893–910.

Chong, Dennis, and Jamie Druckman. "Framing Theory." *Annual Review of Political Science* 10 (2007): 103–26.

Citrin, Jack, and Donald P. Green. "The Self-Interest Motive in American Public Opinion." In *Research in Micropolitics*, edited by Samuel Long, 1–28. Greenwich, CT: JAI Press, 1990.

Converse, Philip E. "The Nature of Belief Systems in Mass Publics." In *Ideology and Discontent*, edited by David E. Apter, 206–31. New York: Free Press, 1964.

Dahl, Robert A. *A Preface to Democratic Theory: How Does Popular Sovereignty Function in America?* Chicago: University of Chicago Press, 1956.

———. *Who Governs? Democracy and Power in an American City*. New Haven, CT: Yale University Press, 1961.

Damasio, Antonio R. *Descartes' Error: Emotion, Reason, and the Human Brain*. New York: Grosset / Putnam Books, 1994.

Delli Carpini, Michael, and Scott Keeter. *What Americans Know About Politics and Why It Matters*. New Haven, CT: Yale University Press, 1996.

Downs, Anthony. *An Economic Theory of Democracy*. New York: Harper and Row, 1957.

Edsall, Thomas, and James V. Grimaldi. "On Nov. 2, GOP Got More Bang for Its Billion, Analysis Shows." *Washington Post*, December 30, 2004, A01.

Exley, Zack. "Stories and Numbers—a Closer Look at Camp Obama." *Huffington Post*, August 29, 2007.

Fairlie, John A. "The Nature of Political Representation, I." *American Political Science Review* 34, no. 2 (1940): 236–48.

———. "The Nature of Political Representation, II." *American Political Science Review* 34, no. 3 (1940): 456–66.

Fenno, Richard. *Home Style: House Members in Their Districts*. Boston: Little, Brown, 1978.

Fiorina, Morris P. "Comment: The Problems with P.P.T." *Journal of Law, Economics and Organization* 6 (1990): 255–61.

———. "Information and Rationality in Elections." In *Information and the Democratic Process*, edited by John Ferejohn and James Kuklinski, 329–42. Urbana: University of Illinois Press, 1990.

———. "Parties, Participation, and Representation in America: Old Theories Face New Realities." In *Political Science: The State of the Discipline*, edited by Ira Katznelson and Helen Milner, 511–41. New York: W. W. Norton and Co., 2003.

———. *Representatives, Roll Calls, and Constituencies*. Lexington, MA: D. C. Heath, 1974.

———. "The Voting Decision: Instrumental and Expressive Aspects." *Journal of Politics* 38 (1976): 390–413.

Fiorina, Morris P., Samuel J. Abrams, and Jeremy C. Pope. *Culture War? The Myth of a Polarized America*. New York: Longman, 2004.

Fisher, Dana R. *Activism, Inc.: How the Outsourcing of Grassroots Campaigns Is Strangling Progressive Politics in America*. Stanford, CA: Stanford University Press, 2006.

Ford, D. H., and Richard M. Lerner. *Developmental Systems Theory: An Integrative Approach*. Newbury Park, CA: Sage Publishers, 1992.

Ford, Martin E. *Motivating Humans: Goals, Emotions, and Personal Agency Beliefs*. Newbury Park, CA: Sage Publications, Inc., 1992.

Frijda, N. H. "The Laws of Emotion." *American Psychologist* 43 (1988): 349–58.

Galston, William. "Political Knowledge, Political Engagement, and Civic Education." *Annual Review of Political Science*, no. 4 (2001): 217–34.

Ganz, Marshall. "Resources and Resourcefulness: Strategic Capacity in the Unionization of California Agriculture, 1959–1966." *American Journal of Sociology* 105, no. 4 (2000): 1003–62.

Ganz, Marshall, Kim Voss, Theresa Sharpe, Carl Somers, and George Strauss. "Against the Tide: Projects and Pathways of the New Generation of Union Leaders, 1984–2001." In *Rebuilding Labor, Organizing and Organizers in the New Union Movement*, edited by Ruth Milkman and Kim Voss, 150–94. Ithaca, NY: Cornell University Press, 2004.

Garofoli, Joe. "Obama Backers Get Neighborly: Campaign Counts on Volunteers Spreading Out Across the State." *San Francisco Chronicle*, January 23, 2008.

Gerber, Alan S., and Donald P. Green. "The Effects of Canvassing, Telephone Calls, and Direct Mail on Voter Turnout: A Field Experiment." *American Political Science Review* 94, no. 3 (2000): 653–63.

Gerber, Alan S., Donald P. Green, and Christopher W. Larimer. "Social Pressure and Voter Turnout: Evidence from a Large-Scale Field Experiment." *American Political Science Review* 102, no. 1 (2008): 33–48.

Gershkoff, Amy R. "Not 'Non-Attitudes,' But Rather 'Non-Measurement.'" Unpublished manuscript. Princeton, NJ, 2004.

Gilens, Martin. "Public Opinion and Democratic Responsiveness: Who Gets What They Want from Government?" Paper presented at the annual meeting of the American Political Science Association, Chicago, 2004.

Golis, Andrew. "The War for Field Organizing." *TPMCafé*, August 29, 2007, http://tpm-cafe.talkingpointsmemo.com/2007/08/29/the_war_for_field_organizing/.

Goodwyn, Lawrence. *The Populist Movement: A Short History of the Agrarian Revolt in America.* New York: Oxford University Press, 1978.

Gould, Lewis L. "Party Conflict: Republicans Versus Democrats, 1877–1901." In *The Gilded Age: Essays on the Origins of Modern America*, edited by Charles Calhoun, 265–80. Lanham, MD: Rowman and Littlefield, 1996.

Gray, Jeffrey A. "The Neuropsychology of Emotion and Personality." In *Cognitive Neurochemistry*, edited by S. M. Stahl, S. D. Iversen, and E. C. Goodman. Oxford: Oxford University Press, 1987.

Green, Donald P., and Ron Shachar. "Habit-Formation and Political Behavior: Evidence of Consuetude in Voter Turnout." *British Journal of Political Science* 30 (2000): 561–73.

Gutmann, Amy. "Identity and Democracy." In *Political Science: State of the Discipline*, edited by Ira Katznelson and Helen Milner, 542–67. New York: American Political Science Association/W. W. Norton, 2002.

Hacker, Jacob S., and Paul Pierson. "Abandoning the Middle: The Bush Tax Cuts and the Limits of Democratic Control." *Perspectives on Politics* 3, no. 1 (2005): 33–53.

Hansen, John Mark. *Gaining Access: Congress and the Farm Lobby, 1919–1981.* Chicago: University of Chicago Press, 1991.

Harris, Frederick C. *Something Within: Religion in African-American Political Activism.* New York: Oxford University Press, 2001.

Haste, H., and Judith Torney-Purta. Introduction to *The Development of Political Understanding: A New Perspective*, edited by H. Haste and Judith Torney-Purta, 1–10. San Francisco: Jossey-Bass, 1992.

Higgins, E. T., and G. King. "Accessibility of Social Constructs: Information-Processing Consequences of Individual and Contextual Variability." In *Personality, Cognition, and Social Interaction*, edited by N. Cantor and J. Kihlstrom, 69–121. Hillsdale, NJ: Erlbaum, 1981.

Hillygus, Sunshine, and Todd Shields. *The Persuadable Voter: Wedge Issues in Presidential Campaigns.* Princeton, NJ: Princeton University Press, 2008.

Hirschman, Albert. *Exit, Voice, and Loyalty.* Cambridge, MA: Harvard University Press, 1972.

Holian, David B., Timothy B. Krebs, and Michael H. Walsh. "Constituency Opinion, Ross Perot, and Roll-Call Behavior in the U.S. House: The Case of the NAFTA." *Legislative Studies Quarterly* 22, no. 3 (1997): 369–92.

Huckfeldt, Robert, and John Sprague. *Citizens, Politics and Social Communication: Information and Influence in an Election Campaign.* Edited by James Kuklinski, Robert Wyer, and Stanley Feldman. Cambridge Studies in Public Opinion and Political Psychology. New York: Cambridge University Press, 1995.

Hutchings, Vincent L. *Public Opinion and Democratic Accountability: How Citizens Learn About Politics.* Princeton, NJ: Princeton University Press, 2003.

Hyman, H. *Political Socialization: A Study in the Psychology of Political Behavior.* Glencoe, IL: Free Press, 1959.

Jennings, M. Kent. "American Political Participation Viewed Through the Lens of the Political Socialization Project." In *Advances in Political Psychology,* edited by Margaret G. Hermann, 1–18. Oxford: Elsevier, 2004.

Jennings, M. Kent, and Ellen Ann Andersen. "The Importance of Social and Political Context: The Case of Aids Activism." *Political Behavior* 25, no. 2 (2003): 177–99.

Jennings, M. Kent, and Richard Niemi. *Generations and Politics.* Princeton, NJ: Princeton University Press, 1981.

———. *Political Character in Adolescence.* Princeton, NJ: Princeton University Press, 1974.

Johnson, Timothy R., Paul J. Wahlbeck, and James F. Spriggs II. "The Influence of Oral Arguments on the U.S. Supreme Court." *American Political Science Review* 100, no. 1 (2006): 99–113.

Jones, Charles O. "Speculative Augmentation in Federal Air Pollution Policy-Making." *Journal of Politics* 36, no. 2 (1974): 438–64.

Kessel, John H. "The Issues in Issue Voting." *American Political Science Review* 66, no. 2 (1972): 459–65.

Key, Vladimir O. *Politics, Parties, and Pressure Groups.* 3rd ed. New York: Thomas Crowell, 1956.

Kingdon, John W. *Congressmen's Voting Decisions.* 2nd ed. New York: Harper and Row, 1981.

Kirlin, Mary. "Adult Civic Engagement: The Role of Adolescent Participation in Overcoming Income and Educational Barriers." Paper presented at the annual meeting of the American Political Science Association, San Francisco, August 30–September 2, 2001.

Komp, Catherine. "Despite Barriers, Displaced New Orleanians Return Home to Vote." *New Standard,* May 19, 2006.

Konigsmark, Anne Rochell. "New Orleans' Upheaval Shows in Vote Results." *USA Today,* April 24, 2006.

Kornbluh, Mark Lawrence. *Why America Stopped Voting: The Decline of Participatory Democracy and the Emergence of Modern American Politics.* New York: New York University Press, 2000.

Krosnick, Jon A. "Government Policy and Citizen Passion: A Study of Issue Publics in Contemporary America." *Political Behavior* 12, no. 1 (1990): 59–92.

———. "The Role of Attitude Importance in Social Evaluation: A Study of Policy Preferences, Presidential Candidate Evaluations, and Voting Behavior." *Journal of Personality and Social Psychology* 55, no. 2 (1988): 196–210.

Krosnick, Jon A., and Shibley Telhami. "Public Attitudes Toward Israel: A Study of the Attentive and Issue Publics." *International Studies Quarterly* 59 (1995): 535–54.

Kuklinski, James H., and Paul Quirk. "Reconsidering the Rational Public: Cognition, Heuristics, and Mass Opinion." In *Elements of Reason,* edited by Arthur Lupia and Matthew D. McCubbins, 153–82. New York: Cambridge University Press, 2000.

Laitin, David D. *Identity in Formation.* Ithaca, NY: Cornell University Press, 1998.

Lane, Richard D., and Lynn Nadel. *Cognitive Neuroscience of Emotion.* New York: Oxford University Press, 2000.

Lane, Robert E. *Political Ideology: Why the Common Man Believes What He Does.* New York: Free Press, 1962.

Lazarus, R. S. "Progress on a Cognitive-Motivational-Relational Theory of Emotion." *American Psychologist* 46 (1991): 819–34.

LeDoux, Joseph E. "Emotional Memory Systems in the Brain." *Behavioral Brain Research* 58 (1993): 68–79.

Leighley, Jan. *Strength in Numbers? The Political Mobilization of Racial and Ethnic Minorities.* Princeton, NJ: Princeton University Press, 2001.

Lohmann, Susanne. "A Signaling Model of Informative and Manipulative Political Action." *American Political Science Review* 87, no. 2 (1993): 319–33.

Lundgren, Kari. "Welcome to the Age of Consumer Politics." *Mother Jones*, September 9, 2004.

Mansbridge, Jane J. "Rethinking Representation." *American Political Science Review* 97, no. 4 (2003): 515–28.

Marcus, George E. *The Sentimental Citizen: Emotion in Democratic Politics.* University Park, PA: Pennsylvania State University Press, 2002.

Marcus, George E., W. Russell Neuman, and Michael B. MacKuen. *Affective Intelligence and Political Judgment.* Chicago: University of Chicago Press, 2000.

Martelle, Scott. "Famed Organizer Sees History in the Making: Veteran Union Activist Marshall Ganz, Who Was There When RFK Was Shot, Is Putting His Passion to Work for Barack Obama Now." *Los Angeles Times*, June 15, 2008.

———. "The Political Machine vs. the Grass Roots." *Los Angeles Times*, September 4, 2007.

Mayhew, David. *Congress: The Electoral Connection.* New Haven, CT: Yale University Press, 1974.

McAdam, Doug. "The Biographical Consequences of Activism." *American Sociological Review* 54, no. 5 (1989): 744–60.

———. *Freedom Summer.* New York: Oxford University Press, 1990.

McClellan, J. A., and J. Youniss. "Two Systems of Youth Service: Determinants of Voluntary and Required Youth Community Service." *Journal of Youth and Adolescence* 32, no. 1 (2003): 47–58.

McGerr, Michael. *Decline of Popular Politics: The American North, 1865–1928.* New York: Oxford University Press, 1986.

Meyer, David S., and Sidney Tarrow. *The Social Movement Society: Contentious Politics for a New Century.* Lanham, MD: Rowman and Littlefield, 1998.

Miller, Joanne M. "Why Do Individuals Participate in Politics?" Paper presented at the annual meeting of the Midwest Political Science Association, Chicago, 2005.

Miller, Joanne M., Jon A. Krosnick, Allyson Holbrook, and Laura Lowe. "The Impact of Policy Change Threat on Financial Contributions to Interest Groups." Unpublished manuscript. University of Minnesota, 2004.

Miller, Joanne M., and Wendy Rahn. "Identity-Based Feelings, Beliefs, and Actions: How Being Influences Doing." Unpublished manuscript. University of Minnesota, 2002.

Miller, Warren E., and Donald E. Stokes. "Constituency Influence in Congress." In *Elections and the Political Order*, edited by Angus Campbell, Philip E. Converse, Warren E. Miller, and Donald E. Stokes, 351–73. New York: Wiley, 1966.

Moreno, Sylvia. "Displaced Voters Make Wishes Known for New Orleans." *Washington Post*, April 12, 2006.

Mutz, Diana. *Impersonal Influence.* Cambridge Studies in Public Opinion and Political Psychology. New York: Cambridge University Press, 1998.

"Nagin Re-elected in Narrow New Orleans Mayoral Race." *PBS Online NewsHour*, May 22, 2006, http://www.pbs.org/newshour/.

Nichols, Bill. "More Voters Aren't Waiting for Election Day: Campaigns Want People at Polls Early." *USA Today*, October 27, 2006, 7A.

Nichols, Hans. "Hill Dems Get into Demzilla." *Hill*, February 17, 2005.

Nickerson, David. "Is Voting Contagious? Evidence from Two Field Experiments." *American Political Science Review* 102 (February 2008): 49–57.

Nie, Norman, Jane Junn, and Kenneth Stehlik-Barry. *Education and Democratic Citizenship in America*. Chicago: University of Chicago Press, 1996.

Niemi, Richard, and Larry M. Bartels. "New Measures of Issue Salience: An Evaluation." *Journal of Politics* 47, no. 4 (1985): 1212–20.

Nisbett, Richard E., and Timothy DeCamp Wilson. "Telling More Than We Can Know: Verbal Reports on Mental Processes." *Psychological Review* 84, no. 3 (1977): 231–59.

Nussbaum, Martha C. *Upheavals of Thought: The Intelligence of Emotions*. New York: Cambridge University Press, 2001.

Olson, Mancur. *The Logic of Collective Action: Public Goods and the Theory of Groups*. Cambridge, MA: Harvard University Press, 1965.

Ostrogorski, M. *Democracy and the Organization of the Political Parties*. Translated by Frederick Clarke. Vol. 2. New York: Macmillan, 1902.

Overbye, Einar. "Making a Case for the Rational, Self-Regarding, Ethical Voter . . . and Solving the Paradox of Not Voting in the Process." *European Journal of Political Research* 27 (1995): 369–96.

Page, Benjamin, and R. Y. Shapiro. "Effects of Public Opinion on Policy." *American Political Science Review* 77 (1983): 175–90.

Patterson, Thomas E. *The Vanishing Voter: Public Involvement in an Age of Uncertainty*. New York: Alfred A. Knopf, 2002.

Pervin, L. A. "Self-Regulation and the Problem of Volition." In *Advances in Motivation and Achievement*, edited by M. L. Maehr and Paul R. Pintrich, 1–20. Greenwich, CT: JAI, 1991.

Petty, R. E., and Jon A. Krosnick, eds. *Attitude Strength: Antecedents and Consequences*. Hillsdale, NJ: Erlbaum, 1995.

Pierson, Paul. "When Effect Becomes Cause: Policy Feedback and Political Change." *World Politics* 45 (1993): 595–628.

Pitkin, Hannah. *The Concept of Representation*. Berkeley: University of California Press, 1967.

Pittman, Thane S. "Motivation." In *The Handbook of Social Psychology*, edited by Daniel T. Gilbert, Susan T. Fiske, and Gardner Lindzey, 549–90. New York: Oxford University Press, 1998.

Plutzer, Eric. "Becoming a Habitual Voter: Inertia, Resources, and Growth in Young Adulthood." *American Political Science Review* 96, no. 1 (2002): 41–56.

Polsby, Nelson, and Aaron Wildavsky. *Presidential Elections: Strategies and Structures of American Politics*. New York: Rowman and Littlefield, 2004.

Price, Vincent, and John Zaller. "Who Gets the News? Alternative Measures of News Reception and Their Implications for Research." *Public Opinion Quarterly* 57, no. 2 (1993): 133–64.

Public Knowledge of Current Affairs Little Changed by News and Information Revolu-

tions: What Americans Know, 1989–2000. Washington, DC: Pew Research Center for People and the Press, 2007.

Putnam, Robert. *Bowling Alone: The Collapse and Revival of American Community.* New York: Simon and Schuster, 2000.

Raum, Tom, and Nedra Pickler. "Obama Seals Nomination: 'This Is Our Moment.'" Associated Press, June 4, 2008.

RePass, David E. "Issue Salience and Party Choice." *American Political Science Review* 65, no. 2 (1971): 389–400.

Riker, William H., and Peter C. Ordeshook. "A Theory of the Calculus of Voting." *American Political Science Review* 62 (1968): 25–42.

Robinson, John Paul, Phillip R. Shaver, and Lawrence S. Wrightsman, eds. *Measures of Political Attitudes.* Measures of Social Psychological Attitudes. New York: Academic Press, 1999.

Rosenstone, Steven J., and John Mark Hansen. *Mobilization, Participation, and Democracy in America.* New York: Macmillan, 1993.

Salisbury, Robert H. "The Urban Party Organization Member." *Public Opinion Quarterly* 29, no. 4 (1965): 550–64.

Sapiro, Virginia. "Not Your Parents' Political Socialization: Introduction for a New Generation." *Annual Review of Political Science* 7 (2004): 1–23.

Schacter, Daniel. *Searching for Memory: The Brain, the Mind, and the Past.* New York: Basic Books, 1997.

Schickler, Eric. *Disjointed Pluralism.* Princeton, NJ: Princeton University Press, 2001.

Schier, Steven. *By Invitation Only: The Rise of Exclusive Politics in the United States.* Pittsburgh: University of Pittsburgh Press, 2000.

Schlesinger, Joseph A. *Political Parties and the Winning of Office.* Chicago: University of Chicago Press, 1991.

———. "The Primary Goals of Political Parties: A Clarification of Positive Theory." *American Political Science Review* 69 (1975): 840–49.

Schlozman, Kay Lehman. "Citizen Participation in America: What Do We Know? Why Do We Care?" In *Political Science: State of the Discipline*, edited by Ira Katznelson and Helen Milner, 433–61. New York: W. W. Norton and Co., 2003.

Schlozman, Kay Lehman, and Sidney Verba. *Injury to Insult: Unemployment, Class, and Political Response.* Cambridge, MA: Harvard University Press, 1979.

Schlozman, Kay Lehman, Sidney Verba, and Henry Brady. "Participation's Not a Paradox: The View from American Activists." *British Journal of Political Science* 25, no. 1 (1995): 1–36.

Schuessler, Alexander A. *A Logic of Expressive Choice.* Princeton, NJ: Princeton University Press, 2000.

Schuman, H., and S. Presser. *Questions and Answers: Experiments on Question Form, Wording, and Context in Attitude Surveys.* New York: Academic Press, 1981.

Shapiro, Catherine R., David W. Brady, Richard Brody, and John Ferejohn. "Linking Constituency Opinion and Senate Voting Scores: A Hybrid Explanation." *Legislative Studies Quarterly* 15, no. 4 (1990): 599–621.

Shepard, Scott. "The Elements of Obama's Successful Campaign." Cox News Service, June 5, 2008.

Skocpol, Theda. *Diminished Democracy: From Membership to Management.* Norman: University of Oklahoma Press, 2003.

————. *Protecting Soldiers and Mothers: The Political Origins of Social Policy in the United States.* Cambridge, MA: Harvard University Press, 1992.

Skocpol, Theda, Marshall Ganz, and Ziad Munson. "A Nation of Organizers: The Institutional Origins of Civic Voluntarism in the United States." *American Political Science Review* 94, no. 3 (2000): 527–46.

Smith, Rogers. *Stories of Peoplehood: The Politics and Morals of Political Membership.* New York: Cambridge University Press, 2003.

Stimson, James A., Michael B. MacKuen, and Robert S. Erikson. "Dynamic Representation." *American Political Science Review* 89, no. 3 (1995): 543–65.

Stoker, Laura, and M. Kent Jennings. "Life-Cycle Transitions and Political Participation: The Case of Marriage." *American Political Science Review* 89 (1995): 421–36.

Strolovitch, Dara. *Affirmative Advocacy: Race, Class, and Gender in Interest Group Politics.* Chicago: University of Chicago Press, 2007.

Taddeo, Lisa. "The Man Who Made Obama." *Esquire*, February 2, 2009.

Task Force on Inequality and American Democracy. *American Democracy in an Age of Rising Inequality.* Washington, DC: American Political Science Association, 2004.

Tate, Katherine. *From Protest to Politics: The New Black Voters in American Elections.* Cambridge, MA: Harvard University Press, 1993.

Teske, Nathan. "Beyond Altruism: Identity-Construction as Moral Motive in Political Explanation." *Political Psychology* 18, no. 1 (1997): 71–91.

————. *Political Activists in America: The Identity Construction Model of Political Participation.* New York: Cambridge University Press, 1997.

Valentino, Nicholas, Vincent Hutchings, and Ismail White. "Cues That Matter: How Political Ads Prime Racial Attitudes During Campaigns." *American Political Science Review* 96, no. 1 (2002): 75–90.

Verba, Sidney, and Norman Nie. *Participation in America: Political Democracy and Social Equality.* New York: Harper and Row, 1972.

Verba, Sidney, Kay Lehman Schlozman, and Henry Brady. *Voice and Equality: Civic Voluntarism in American Politics.* Cambridge, MA: Harvard University Press, 1995.

Visser, Penny S., Jon A. Krosnick, and Joseph P. Simmons. "Distinguishing the Cognitive and Behavioral Consequences of Attitude Importance and Certainty: A New Approach to Testing the Common-Factor Hypothesis." *Journal of Experimental and Social Psychology* 39 (2003): 118–41.

Waldman, Paul. "The Myth of the Rational Iowa Voter." *American Prospect*, October 3, 2007, http://www.prospect.org/cs/articles?article=the_myth_of_the_rational_iowa_voter.

Walker, Jack. "Interests, Political Parties, and Policy Formation in American Democracy." In *Federal Social Policy: The Historical Dimension*, edited by D. T. Critchlow and E. W. Hawley, 141–70. University Park, PA: Penn State University Press, 1988.

Walker, Jack L., Jr. *Mobilizing Interest Groups in America: Patrons, Professions, and Social Movements.* Ann Arbor: University of Michigan Press, 1991.

Weigel, David. "The Political Bull's-Eye: Persuading the Right People with Microtargeting." *Campaigns and Elections*, February 2006.

Weiner, B. "History of Motivational Research in Education." *Journal of Educational Psychology* 82 (1990): 616–22.

Weir, Margaret, and Marshall Ganz. "Reconnecting People and Politics." In *The New Majority: Toward a Popular Progressive Politics*, edited by Stanley B. Greenberg and Theda Skocpol, 149–71. New Haven, CT: Yale University Press, 1997.

Weissberg, Robert. "Collective Versus Dyadic Representation in Congress." *American Political Science Review* 72 (1978): 535–47.

Wiebe, Robert. *The Search for Order: 1877–1920*. Santa Barbara, CA: Greenwood Publishing Group, 1967.

Willingham, Daniel. "A Neuropsychological Theory of Motor Skill Learning." *Psychological Review* 105 (1998): 558–84.

Wilson, James Q. *The Amateur Democrat*. Chicago: University of Chicago Press, 1962.

———. *Political Organizations*. New York: Basic Books, 1973.

Wolfinger, Raymond E. "The Rational Citizen Faces Election Day, or What Rational Choice Theorists Don't Tell You About American Elections." In *Elections at Home and Abroad: Essays in Honor of Warren E. Miller*, edited by M. Kent Jennings and Thomas E. Mann, 71–89. Ann Arbor: University of Michigan Press, 1994.

Wolfinger, Raymond E., and Steven J. Rosenstone. *Who Votes?* New Haven, CT: Yale University Press, 1980.

Woodwell, William H. *Thinking Outside the Ballot Box: Innovations for the Polling Place*. Washington, DC: League of Women Voters Education Fund, 2006.

Wright, Gerald C. "Policy Voting in the U.S. Senate: Who Is Represented?" *Legislative Studies Quarterly* 14, no. 4 (1989): 465–86.

Youniss, James, and Miranda Yates. *Community Service and Social Responsibility in Youth*. Chicago: University of Chicago Press, 1997.

Youniss, James, Jeffrey A. McLellan, and Miranda Yates. "What We Know About Engendering Civic Identity." *American Behavioral Scientist* 40, no. 5 (1997): 620–31.

Zajonc, Robert B. "Emotions." In *The Handbook of Social Psychology*, edited by Daniel T. Gilbert, Susan T. Fiske, and Gardner Lindzey, 591–634. New York: Oxford University Press, 1998.

Zaller, John. *The Nature and Origin of Mass Opinion*. New York: Cambridge University Press, 1992.

Zuckerman, Alan S. *The Social Logic of Politics: Personal Networks as Contexts for Political Behavior*. Philadelphia: Temple University Press, 2005.

Index

Page numbers in *italics* indicate tabular and figurative material. Pseudonyms used for individuals in the author's study may be found under Political Pathways study (2008).

National Purpose, Local Action
study (2003), 116–19, *118*, 159
emotion, motivation, and participation,
13–14
advertising's power to arouse, 45
cognition and emotion, 162n34,
164n37
conscious and unconscious emotional
processing, 164n33
critical functions served by emotion,
165n40
goal orientation and, 17, 35–36, 38–40
in literature, 26
socialization, political, 96
encouraging political participation,
128–48
by civic and political organizations,
133–43, *136*
activation models, 134–37, *136*
mobilization models, 137–43
role of, 146–47
future research on, 143–45
Iowa caucus, percentage of eligible
voters participating in, 128–29
issue publics hypothesis and,
130–33
knowledge of politics, American lack
of, 48, 55
political reform and, 145–48
populist movement of 1890s, lessons
from, 139–43
equality. *See* inequality
evangelical churches, political motivation
in, 16, 20
ExCom Leader Survey (ELS), Sierra Club
National Purpose, Local Action
study (2003), 116–19, *118*, 159
extremity, 52–53

farmers' involvement in populist movement, 139–40
farmworkers, political motivation of,
23–26, 34, 39
fear, evocations of, 45
Fiorina, Morris, 7, 30, 31
Ford, D. H., 164n36
framing, 45

Gage, Alex, 135–36
Ganz, Marshall, 97
Gates, Bill, 105
Gay-Straight Alliance, 110
Gerber, Alan, 37
Gershkoff, Amy R., 166–67n26
get-out-the-vote (GOTV) efforts, 134–35
Giuliani, Rudy, 129
"giving back" as motivation, 103–4
goal-oriented approach to motivation/
participation
alternative goals leading to participation and then issue commitment,
113–19
cost-benefit or rational choice theory,
29–32
delayed gratification, 32–33
dynamic and interactive nature of, 34
Goodwyn, Lawrence, 139, 140
GOP Voter Vault, 134, 135
GOTV (get-out-the-vote) efforts, 134–35
Great Society reforms, 146
Green, Donald, 37
group identity, 45, 54

Hansen, John Mark, 28, 31
Harris, Frederick, 37
Haste, Helen, 95
homeland security, 53
Huckabee, Mike, 129
Hunter, Christopher, 136
Hurricane Katrina disaster, New Orleans
mayoral election following, 1–4, 8–9,
12, 86, 132
Hutchings, Vincent, 51, 52, 94–95,
168n8

identity, 45, 54
Identity Construction Model, 95–96
immigrant rights, 51–52, 110–11
income. *See* wealth
inequality
activation model reinforcing, *136*,
136–37
encouraging participation of underprivileged persons. *See* encouraging political participation